EASY
KANA
WORKBOOK

Basic Practice in Hiragana and Katakana
for Japanese Language Students

Rita L. Lampkin
and
Osamu Hoshino

McGraw Hill

New York   Chicago   San Francisco   Lisbon   London   Madrid   Mexico City
Milan   New Delhi   San Juan   Seoul   Singapore   Sydney   Toronto

About the Authors

Rita Lampkin is a graduate of Brigham Young University—Hawaii Campus and a veteran of more than sixteen years teaching Japanese. While living in Japan she was a full-time employee of Nippon Electric Company. Her Japanese teaching experience includes three years both teaching and developing materials for intensive courses in Hawaii. She developed and taught a course in basic Japanese for employees of Disneyland in Anaheim, California, and currently teaches at Mt. San Antonio College in Walnut, California.

Osamu Hoshino also graduated from BYU—Hawaii Campus, where he and Ms. Lampkin first collaborated in teaching Japanese and developing course materials. He then moved to BYU's main campus at Provo, Utah, where he received an MPA while teaching at the Missionary Training Center there. A native of Japan, he has taught English as a second language in his home country. He has since taken American citizenship and settled in Salt Lake City, Utah, where he is Director of the Utah State Department of Economic Development.

The *McGraw·Hill* Companies

Copyright © 1991 by The McGraw-Hill Companies, Inc. All rights reserved. Printed in the United States of America. Except as permitted under the United States Copyright Act of 1976, no part of this publication may be reproduced or distributed in any form or by any means, or stored in a database or retrieval system, without the prior written permission of the publisher.

17 18 19 20 21 22 23 24 25 26 27 28 29 30 31   VRS/VRS   0 9 8 7

ISBN-13: 978-0-8442-8532-0
ISBN-10:   0-8442-8532-3

McGraw-Hill books are available at special quantity discounts to use as premiums and sales promotions, or for use in corporate training programs. For more information, please write to the Director of Special Sales, Professional Publishing, McGraw-Hill, Two Penn Plaza, New York, NY 10121-2298. Or contact your local bookstore.

This book is printed on acid-free paper.

CONTENTS

Introduction

This practical workbook is for all students of Japanese who want to learn the basic phonetic writing systems in use by the Japanese. This workbook is a self-contained course, which can be used both for independent study or in the classroom. It can also serve as an ideal supplement to any basic conversation course in Japanese.

Both the hiragana and katakana sections of this workbook provide plenty of practice in writing characters, words, and sentences. In addition, each section concludes with a practice and self-test.

At the back of the book are several useful appendices, including complete hiragana and katakana charts as well as answers and translations to the practice and self-tests.

The *EASY KANA WORKBOOK* combines a systematic approach with ample practice and the reinforcement necessary to master both reading and writing hiragana and katakana.

OVERVIEW

THE THREE JAPANESE WRITING SYSTEMS

There are three kinds of characters involved in writing Japanese:

1. KANJI
2. KATAKANA
3. HIRAGANA

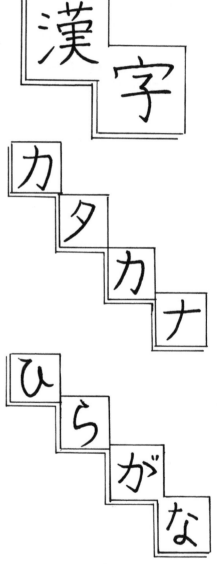

1. **KANJI** is a set of ideographs and pictographs borrowed originally from the Chinese and adapted to fit the Japanese language.

    Each *KANJI* character carries a specific meaning and may be pronounced several different ways, depending on its use. There are over 1800 *KANJI* in common use, plus a good number of less frequently used or archaic characters.

2. **KATAKANA** is a strictly phonetic system. That is, each character represents a particular sound, with no inherent meaning.

    KATAKANA is used to write, as closely as the limited Japanese sound system will allow, words and names of foreign origin. It is also used to place emphasis on or call attention to a particular word or phrase and is used liberally in advertising.

    There are 46 basic characters in the *KATAKANA* system, plus a number of "combination characters" (contracted characters) and "sound change characters."

3. **HIRAGANA** is also strictly phonetic, has the same number of characters as the *KATAKANA* system, and represents the same set of sounds. The only difference between the two systems is in their use.

    HIRAGANA is used to write particles, verb endings, conjunctions, etc.—all the words or parts of words that are not represented in *KATAKANA* or *KANJI*.

    The two sets of phonetic characters (*HIRAGANA* and *KATAKANA*) are known collectively as *KANA*.

Since the *KANA* symbols are strictly phonetic, they may be used to write any word for which *KANJI* is not customarily used, or for which the *KANJI* is not known to the writer. For these purposes, *HIRAGANA* is ordinarily used, rather than *KATAKANA*.

Japanese children usually are taught first *HIRAGANA* and then *KATAKANA,* while concurrently studying some of the simpler *KANJI*. The same order will be used in this course as well.

The three Japanese writing systems—*HIRAGANA, KATAKANA,* and *KANJI*—are used in combination with each other, as shown in the following example sentence:

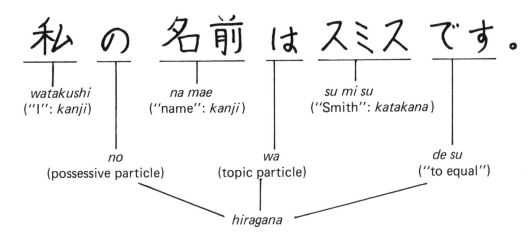

WATAKUSHI NO NAMAE WA SUMISU DESU.   =   My name is Smith.

Japanese may be written horizontally, from left to right, like English, or from top to bottom vertically, beginning at the right side of the page and moving toward the left. There are rare occasions when you may see it written horizontally from right to left. On a vehicle, for example, an advertisement or identification will be written from the front of the vehicle towards the rear, making it read left to right on one side and right to left on the other.

ABOUT RŌMAJI
(The Roman Alphabet)

Over the last century several systems of romanization have been developed to represent the Japanese sound system. There have even been attempts at a permanent substitution of *RŌMAJI* for the much more difficult *KANJI* system, although there has never been enough popular support to bring the idea to reality. One of the major problems in making such a substitution is the fact that the Japanese sound system is extremely limited, making homonyms—words that sound alike but have different meanings—the rule, rather than the exception. Since *KANJI* characters illustrate the meaning of the words they represent, they help to clarify what is being written.

Still, many Japanese conversation texts use one or another of the various *RŌMAJI* systems, since learning Japanese as a second language by way of *KANA* and *KANJI* exclusively is a slow, difficult process.

HIRAGANA NO GOJŪON

(The 50 Sounds of HIRAGANA)

The word *GOJŪON* literally means "fifty sounds," although the modern system of *KANA* actually consists of only 46 symbols.

Note that the characters in the chart below represent syllables, rather than individual sounds as in the Roman alphabet. For this reason the set of symbols is called a SYLLABARY.

A syllable in the Japanese system may be a single vowel sound *(A, I, U, E,* or *O)* or a consonant-vowel combination, such as *KA* or *TSU* or *CHI.* The only exception is the soft consonant *N′* (ん), which is also considered a single syllable.

Note also that this chart is presented in vertical order, beginning in the upper right-hand corner and moving downward and across the page toward the left. This is the order in which words are given in a *KANA* dictionary, just as words are given in A-B-C order in a dictionary using the Roman alphabet. When you memorize these characters, you should memorize them in order.

Begin here. ↓

わ WA	ら RA	や YA	ま MA	は HA	な NA	た TA	さ SA	か KA	あ A
	り RI		み MI	ひ HI	に NI	ち CHI	し SHI	き KI	い I
	る RU	ゆ YU	む MU	ふ FU	ぬ NU	つ TSU	す SU	く KU	う U
	れ RE		め ME	へ HE	ね NE	て TE	せ SE	け KE	え E
を (W)O	ろ RO	よ YO	も MO	ほ HO	の NO	と TO	そ SO	こ KO	お O
ん N′									

This chart is given in machine-made characters in Appendix A.

WRITING CHARACTERS

The exercises on the following pages are intended not only to help you learn to recognize and write the *HIRAGANA* characters, but to help you to develop good penmanship. Keep the following points in mind as you carry out the exercises presented.

1. For the purpose of writing practice, each character is presented within a square. Notice that the character is always more or less CENTERED IN ITS SQUARE. In normal circumstances, of course, the squares are absent; but the characters should still be spaced as if written in a row or column of squares. Closer spacing of the characters may make your writing difficult to read.

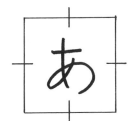

2. In English and many other languages, it is considered appropriate to slant letters or to add extra curlicues and swashes, according to the handwriting style of the individual. In Japanese, however, THE CHARACTERS SHOULD BE WRITTEN AS SHOWN, UPRIGHT and with no more slant, curl, or swash than is shown for each character. Slanting a *KANA* character may make it look like some other character and become difficult to read.

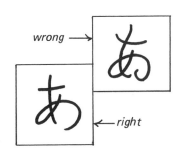

wrong →

← *right*

3. You should realize that *KANA* and *KANJI* were originally created when brush-and-ink was the normal writing medium. The brush was held upright in the hand, rather than at an angle as a pen or pencil would be used. It may help your penmanship if you TRY HOLDING YOUR PEN UPRIGHT as you write the characters.

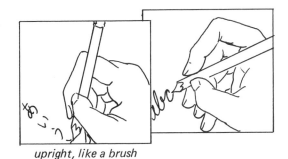

upright, like a brush

4. Pay careful attention to the STROKE ORDER and STROKE DIRECTION indicated by the numbers and arrows, as these are essential to correct formation of each character. Note that basic stroke order moves from left to right and top to bottom, although there are occasional variations. Also, horizontal strokes are ordinarily written before vertical strokes.

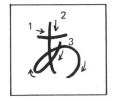

5. TAKE YOUR TIME with these exercises. Don't rush through them, but use them to develop good writing habits and penmanship.

First, TRACE each character several times, paying strict attention to stroke order and direction. Then carefully draw the character in the blank squares. Take your time. Develop good habits NOW.

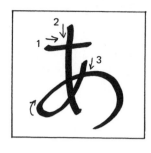

A   as in FATHER

あ あ あ あ あ あ あ あ あ
あ あ あ あ あ あ あ あ あ

I   as in MACHINE

い い い い い い い い い
い い い い い い い い い

U   as in RECUPERATE

う う う う う う う う う
う う う う う う う う う

E   as in BETTER

え え え え え え え え え
え え え え え え え

O   as in COOPERATE

お お お お お お お お お

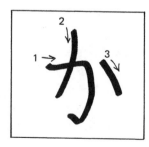

KA

か か か か か か か か か

First, **TRACE** each character several times, paying strict attention to stroke order and direction. Then carefully draw the character in the blank squares. Take your time. Develop good habits NOW.

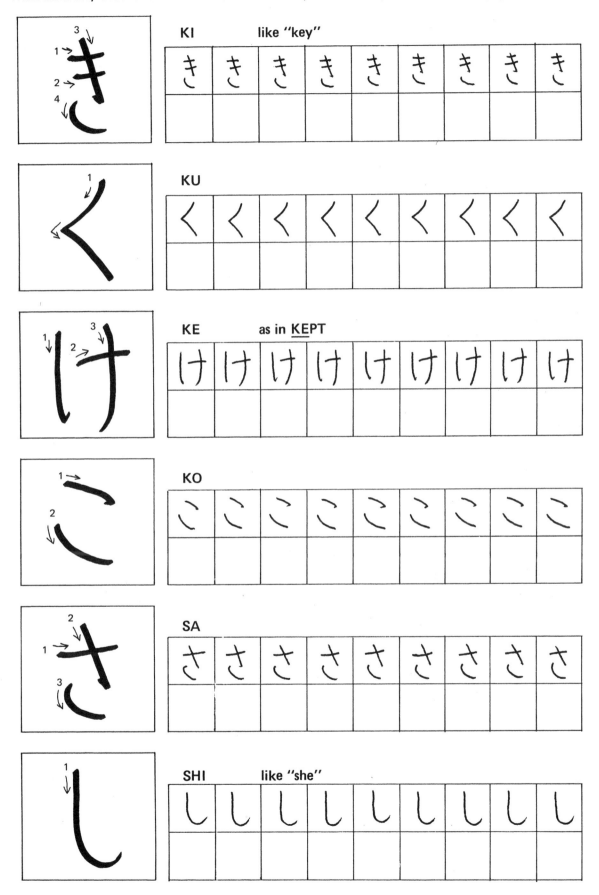

KI like "key"

KU

KE as in <u>KEPT</u>

KO

SA

SHI like "she"

First, **TRACE** each character several times, paying strict attention to stroke order and direction.
Then carefully draw the character in the blank squares. Take your time. Develop good habits NOW.

SU

SE   as in **SETTLE**

SO

TA

CHI   as in **CHEEK**

TSU

First, **TRACE** each character several times, paying strict attention to stroke order and direction.
Then carefully draw the character in the blank squares. Take your time. Develop good habits NOW.

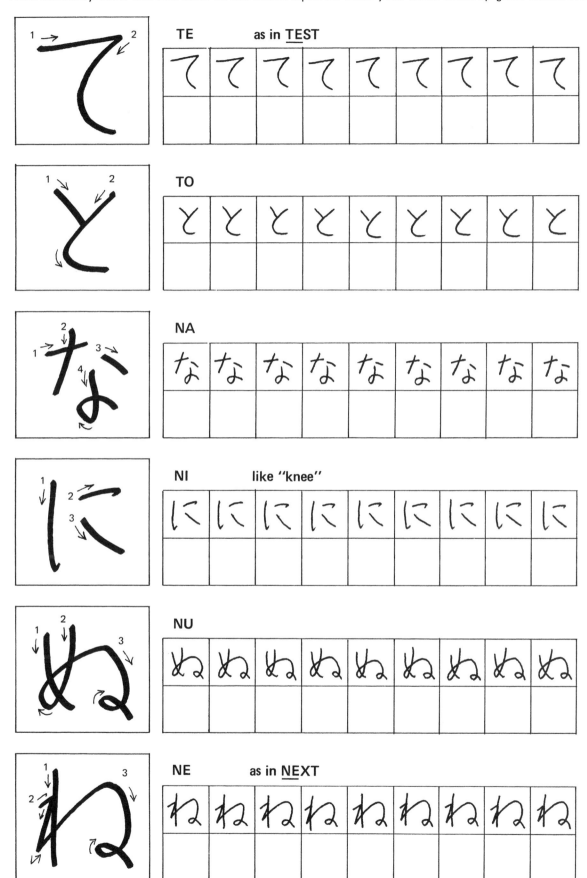

TE   as in **TEST**

TO

NA

NI   like "knee"

NU

NE   as in **NEXT**

First, **TRACE** each character several times, paying strict attention to stroke order and direction. Then carefully draw the character in the blank squares. Take your time. Develop good habits NOW.

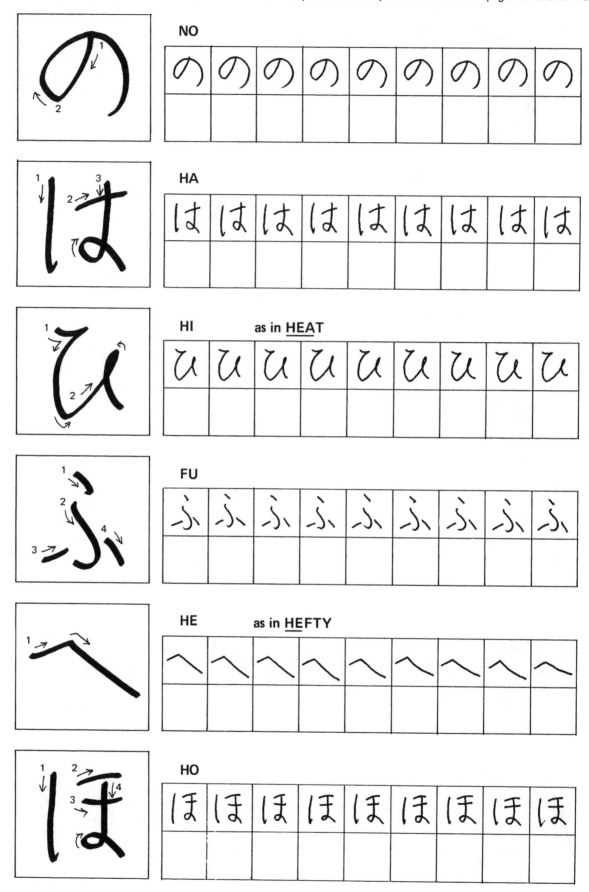

NO

HA

HI   as in **HEAT**

FU

HE   as in **HEFTY**

HO

First, **TRACE** each character several times, paying strict attention to stroke order and direction. Then carefully draw the character in the blank squares. Take your time. Develop good habits NOW.

MA

ま	ま	ま	ま	ま	ま	ま	ま	ま

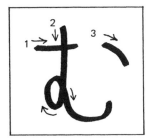

MI   as in <u>MEEK</u>

み	み	み	み	み	み	み	み	み

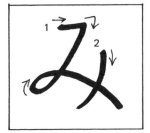

MU

む	む	む	む	む	む	む	む	む

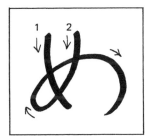

ME   as in <u>MET</u>

め	め	め	め	め	め	め	め	め

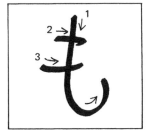

MO

も	も	も	も	も	も	も	も	も

YA

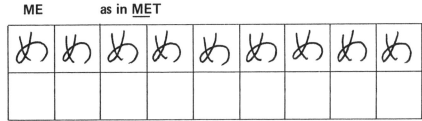

First, **TRACE** each character several times, paying strict attention to stroke order and direction.
Then carefully draw the character in the blank squares. Take your time. Develop good habits NOW.

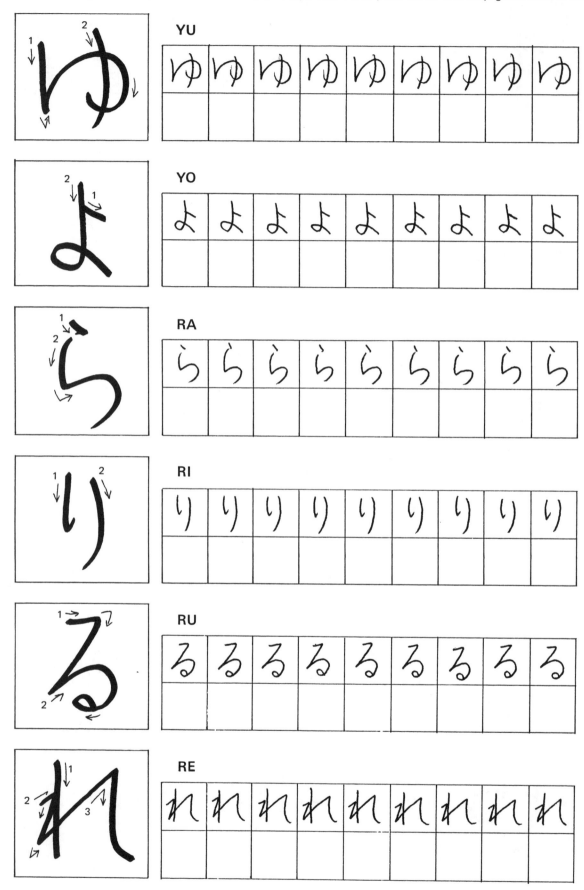

YU

YO

RA

RI

RU

RE

First, **TRACE** each character several times, paying strict attention to stroke order and direction.
Then carefully draw the character in the blank squares. Take your time. Develop good habits NOW.

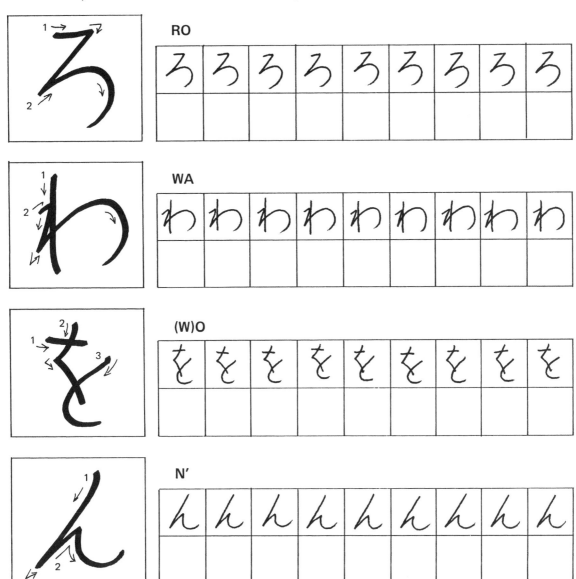

RO

WA

(W)O

N'

VOICED CONSONANTS vs. VOICELESS CONSONANTS

Besides the basic sounds of the *GOJŪON*, there are variations of some of these syllables, made by changing a VOICELESS consonant to a VOICED consonant.

To illustrate what is meant by VOICED and VOICELESS consonants, first put your hand on your throat so that your palm is against the Adam's apple, as in the illustration at right. Now, say the following consonant sounds (just the sound of the letter, not the letter's name):

/G/   (as in GOOD)

/Z/   (as in ZIPPER)

/D/   (as in DARLING)

Notice the vibration that you feel when you pronounce each of these VOICED consonants, so named because they are made by vibrating the vocal cords.

Now pronounce the VOICELESS counterparts of the same consonant sounds:

   /K/   (as in KOALA)   /S/   (as in SOCKS)   /T/   (as in TAPE)

Notice the lack of vibration from the vocal cords when these sounds are pronounced. Notice also that there is no other difference in the way each pair of sounds is pronounced: /G/ is the voiced counterpart of /K/, /Z/ is the voiced counterpart of /S/, and /D/ is the voiced counterpart of /T/. The mouth, lips, and tongue are in the same position for each pair; only the vocalization is different.

Now take a look at the *GOJŪON* chart again:

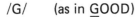

わ WA	ら RA	や YA	ま MA	は HA	な NA	た TA	さ SA	か KA	あ A
	り RI		み MI	ひ HI	に NI	ち CHI	し SHI	き KI	い I
	る RU	ゆ YU	む MU	ふ FU	ぬ NU	つ TSU	す SU	く KU	う U
	れ RE		め ME	へ HE	ね NE	て TE	せ SE	け KE	え E
を (W)O	ろ RO	よ YO	も MO	ほ HO	の NO	と TO	そ SO	こ KO	お O
ん N'									

The arrows indicate three columns of syllables that begin with VOICELESS CONSONANTS. These VOICELESS CONSONANTS can be changed to VOICED CONSONANTS by the use of a symbol called *NIGORI* or *TEN-TEN* (meaning "point-point"), placed to the upper right of the voiceless character, as in the chart on the next page.

た TA — だ DA	さ SA — ざ ZA	か KA — が GA
ち CHI — ぢ JI	し SHI — じ JI	き KI — ぎ GI
つ TSU — づ ZU	す SU — ず ZU	く KU — ぐ GU
て TE — で DE	せ SE — ぜ ZE	け KE — げ GE
と TO — ど DO	そ SO — ぞ ZO	こ KO — ご GO

See how KA （か） becomes GA （が）, SA （さ） becomes ZA （ざ）, TA （た） becomes DA （だ）, etc.

NOTE:

1.   Reason would tell us that the sound /SH/, as in the syllable SHI （し）, when voiced, would become /ZH/, as in the words "measure" and "treasure." However, the /ZH/ sound does not exist in Japanese. The consonant sound represented in the character じ is /J/ as in "John" and "joke."

2.   The syllable CHI （ち）, when voiced, becomes JI, the same syllable represented by the character じ. When writing in KANA, remember that じ is the character most often used to represent the syllable JI. ぢ is used only rarely, and under particular circumstances. For the purposes of the beginner, it is best to use the character じ unless specifically instructed otherwise.

3.   Notice that both ず and づ represent the syllable ZU. The character used most often for this syllable is ず, the other being used only rarely and under particular circumstances. Again, for the beginner, it is best to use the character ず unless specifically instructed otherwise. *(Appendix B includes some common words that call for ぢ and づ instead of じ and ず.)*

VOICED AND VOICELESS BILABIALS

A BILABIAL is a sound made with the lips touching each other. Japanese contains three such bilabials— /M/, /B/, and /P/. The syllables MA, MI, MU, ME, and MO are included in the basic GOJŪON chart. The other bilabials are represented in HIRAGANA and romanization as follows:

ば BA	ぱ PA
び BI	ぴ PI
ぶ BU	ぷ PU
べ BE	ぺ PE
ぼ BO	ぽ PO

Notice that the voiced syllables BA, BI, BU, BE, and BO are represented by the characters for HA, HI, FU, HE, and HO, accompanied by the usual NIGORI points.

The voiceless bilabial syllables PA, PI, PU, PE, and PO are the same basic characters, accompanied by a small circle, called MARU (meaning "circle") or HANDAKU.

Use the following exercises to learn to write the voiced and HANDAKU characters, paying careful attention to stroke order and direction as shown. Again, DO NOT RUSH these exercises; instead, draw the characters carefully in order to develop good penmanship and correct writing habits.

First, **TRACE** each character several times, paying strict attention to stroke order and direction. Then carefully draw the character in the blank squares. Take your time. Develop good habits NOW.

GA

が	が	が	が	が	が	が	が	が

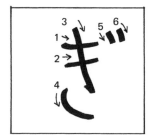

GI   **as in AGGIE**

ぎ	ぎ	ぎ	ぎ	ぎ	ぎ	ぎ	ぎ	ぎ

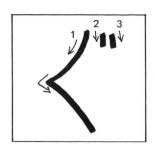

GU

ぐ	ぐ	ぐ	ぐ	ぐ	ぐ	ぐ	ぐ	ぐ

GE   **as in GET**

げ	げ	げ	げ	げ	げ	げ	げ	げ

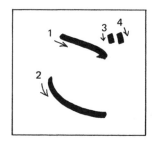

GO

ご	ご	ご	ご	ご	ご	ご	ご	ご

ZA

ざ	ざ	ざ	ざ	ざ	ざ	ざ	ざ	ざ

First, **TRACE** each character several times, paying strict attention to stroke order and direction. Then carefully draw the character in the blank squares. Take your time. Develop good habits NOW.

JI as in JEEP

じ	じ	じ	じ	じ	じ	じ	じ	じ

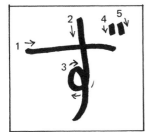

ZU

ず	ず	ず	ず	ず	ず	ず	ず	ず

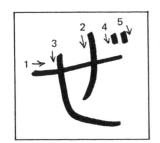

ZE as in ZEPHYR

ぜ	ぜ	ぜ	ぜ	ぜ	ぜ	ぜ	ぜ	ぜ

ZO

ぞ	ぞ	ぞ	ぞ	ぞ	ぞ	ぞ	ぞ	ぞ

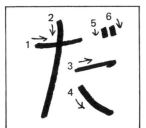

DA

だ	だ	だ	だ	だ	だ	だ	だ	だ

JI as in JEEP

ぢ	ぢ	ぢ	ぢ	ぢ	ぢ	ぢ	ぢ	ぢ

First, **TRACE** each character several times, paying strict attention to stroke order and direction. Then carefully draw the character in the blank squares. Take your time. Develop good habits NOW.

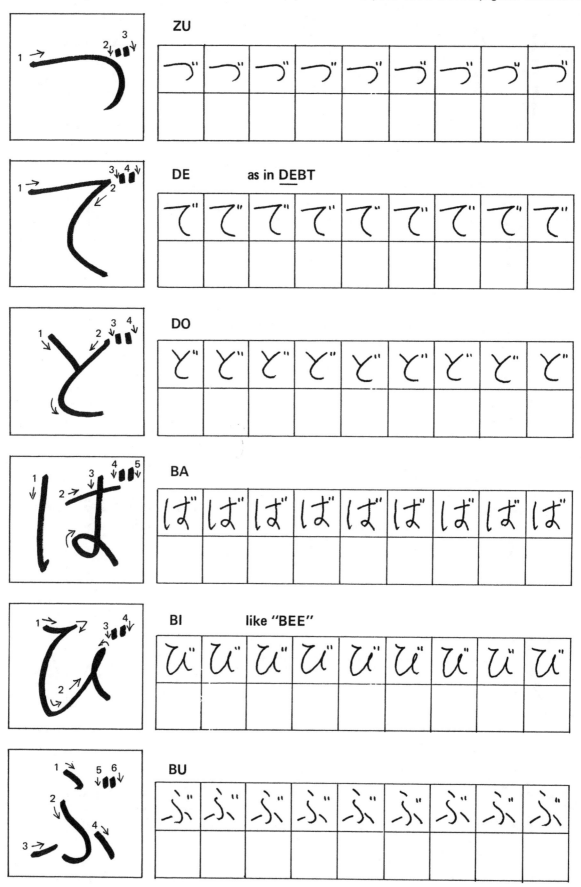

ZU

DE   as in <u>DEBT</u>

DO

BA

BI   like "BEE"

BU

First, **TRACE** each character several times, paying strict attention to stroke order and direction. Then carefully draw the character in the blank squares. Take your time. Develop good habits NOW.

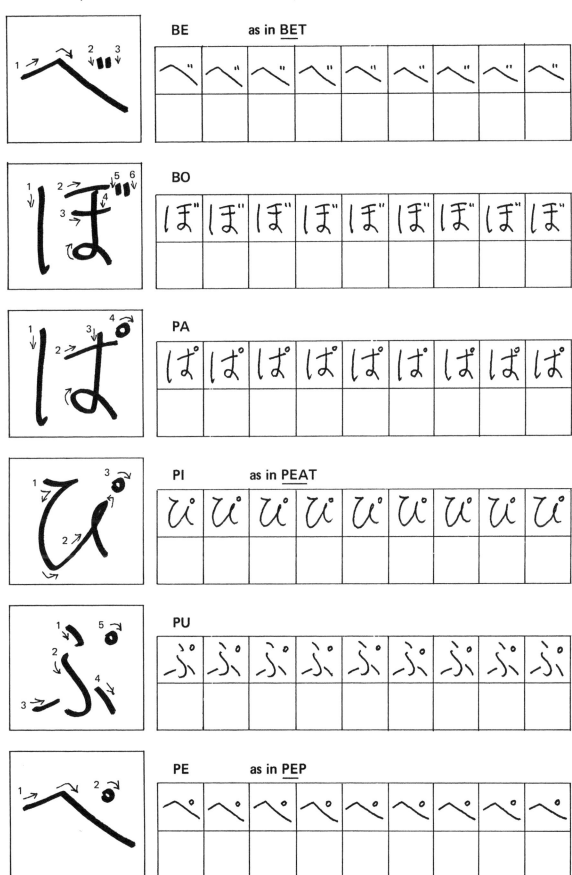

BE   as in BET

BO

PA

PI   as in PEAT

PU

PE   as in PEP

First, **TRACE** each character several times, paying strict attention to stroke order and direction. Then carefully draw the character in the blank squares. Take your time. Develop good habits NOW.

PO

ぽ	ぽ	ぽ	ぽ	ぽ	ぽ	ぽ	ぽ	ぽ

COMBINATION CHARACTERS

(Contracted Syllables)

Take a look at the *GOJŪON* chart at right, particularly the characters in bold script. When these characters are combined with a smaller version of the characters for *YA* (や), *YU* (ゆ), and *YO* (よ) (indicated by the arrow), they form what are called COMBINATION CHARACTERS, as shown in the chart below.

わ WA	ら RA	や YA	ま MA	は HA	な NA	た TA	さ SA	か KA	あ A
	り RI		**み** MI	**ひ** HI	**に** NI	**ち** CHI	**し** SHI	**き** KI	い I
	る RU	ゆ YU	む MU	ふ FU	ぬ NU	つ TSU	す SU	く KU	う U
	れ RE		め ME	へ HE	ね NE	て TE	せ SE	け KE	え E
を (W)O	ろ RO	よ YO	も MO	ほ HO	の NO	と TO	そ SO	こ KO	お O
ん N'		↑							

This chart is given in machine-made characters in Appendix A.

きゃ KYA	しゃ SHA	ちゃ CHA	にゃ NYA	ひゃ HYA	みゃ MYA	りゃ RYA
きゅ KYU	しゅ SHU	ちゅ CHU	にゅ NYU	ひゅ HYU	みゅ MYU	りゅ RYU
きょ KYO	しょ SHO	ちょ CHO	にょ NYO	ひょ HYO	みょ MYO	りょ RYO

This chart is given in machine-made characters in Appendix A.

These combined characters have the value of one syllable each, as compared with two separate syllables when the characters are written the same size, separately. Note the differences in the following examples:

SHIYA "field of vision"   しや   vs.   *SHA* "gauze"   しゃ

KIYU "imaginary fears"   きゆ   vs.   *KYU* "sphere," "globe"   きゅ

RIYOKU "greed"   りよく   vs.   *RYOKUCHA* "green tea"   りょくちゃ

Of course, the voiceless combination characters also have voiced and bilabialized counterparts, represented as before by the accompanying *NIGORI* and *HANDAKU*, as shown in the following chart:

ぎゃ GYA	じゃ JA	ぢゃ JA	びゃ BYA	ぴゃ PYA
ぎゅ GYU	じゅ JU	ぢゅ JU	びゅ BYU	ぴゅ PYU
ぎょ GYO	じょ JO	ぢょ JO	びょ BYO	ぴょ PYO

Note that there two sets of characters for the sounds *JA, JU,* and *JO.* As before, the characters used most often are じゃ , じゅ , and じょ . It is best to use these characters unless otherwise instructed.

This chart is given in machine-made characters in Appendix A.

Use the following exercises to learn to write the combination characters, paying careful attention, as always, to stroke order and direction as shown. DO NOT RUSH. Use these exercises to develop good writing habits and penmanship.

First, **TRACE** each character several times, then carefully draw the character in the blank squares.

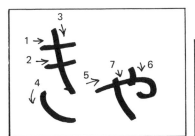

KYA

きゃ	きゃ	きゃ	きゃ	きゃ	きゃ

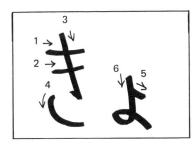

KYU

きゅ	きゅ	きゅ	きゅ	きゅ	きゅ

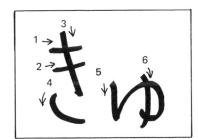

KYO

きょ	きょ	きょ	きょ	きょ	きょ

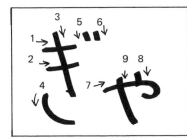

GYA

ぎゃ	ぎゃ	ぎゃ	ぎゃ	ぎゃ	ぎゃ

First, **TRACE** each character several times, paying strict attention to stroke order and direction. Then carefully draw the character in the blank squares. Take your time. Develop good habits NOW.

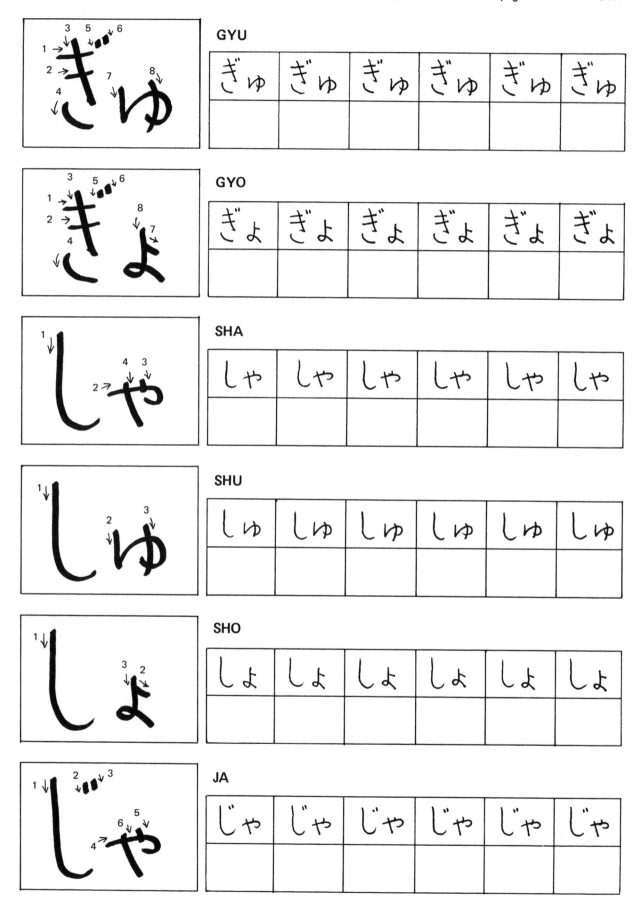

GYU

ぎゅ ぎゅ ぎゅ ぎゅ ぎゅ ぎゅ

GYO

ぎょ ぎょ ぎょ ぎょ ぎょ ぎょ

SHA

しゃ しゃ しゃ しゃ しゃ しゃ

SHU

しゅ しゅ しゅ しゅ しゅ しゅ

SHO

しょ しょ しょ しょ しょ しょ

JA

じゃ じゃ じゃ じゃ じゃ じゃ

First, **TRACE** each character several times, paying strict attention to stroke order and direction. Then carefully draw the character in the blank squares. Take your time. Develop good habits NOW.

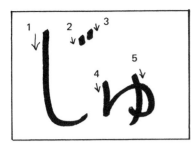

JU

じゅ	じゅ	じゅ	じゅ	じゅ	じゅ

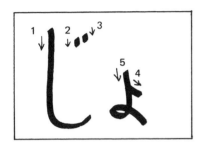

JO

じょ	じょ	じょ	じょ	じょ	じょ

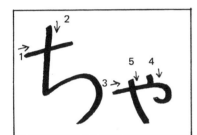

CHA

ちゃ	ちゃ	ちゃ	ちゃ	ちゃ	ちゃ

CHU

ちゅ	ちゅ	ちゅ	ちゅ	ちゅ	ちゅ

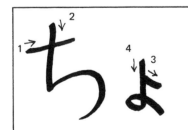

CHO

ちょ	ちょ	ちょ	ちょ	ちょ	ちょ

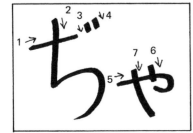

JA

ぢゃ	ぢゃ	ぢゃ	ぢゃ	ぢゃ	ぢゃ

First, **TRACE** each character several times, paying strict attention to stroke order and direction. Then carefully draw the character in the blank squares. Take your time. Develop good habits NOW.

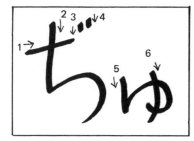

JU

ぢゅ	ぢゅ	ぢゅ	ぢゅ	ぢゅ	ぢゅ

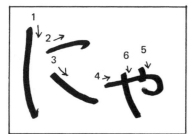

JO

ぢょ	ぢょ	ぢょ	ぢょ	ぢょ	ぢょ

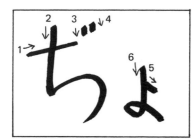

NYA

にゃ	にゃ	にゃ	にゃ	にゃ	にゃ

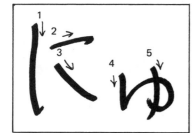

NYU

にゅ	にゅ	にゅ	にゅ	にゅ	にゅ

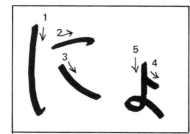

NYO

にょ	にょ	にょ	にょ	にょ	にょ

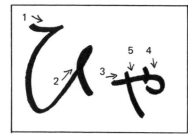

HYA

ひゃ	ひゃ	ひゃ	ひゃ	ひゃ	ひゃ

First, **TRACE** each character several times, paying strict attention to stroke order and direction.
Then carefully draw the character in the blank squares. Take your time. Develop good habits NOW.

HYU

ひゅ	ひゅ	ひゅ	ひゅ	ひゅ	ひゅ

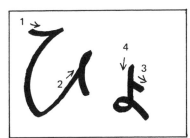

HYO

ひょ	ひょ	ひょ	ひょ	ひょ	ひょ

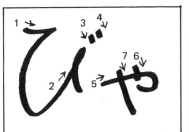

BYA

びゃ	びゃ	びゃ	びゃ	びゃ	びゃ

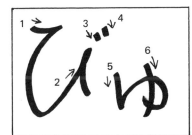

BYU

びゅ	びゅ	びゅ	びゅ	びゅ	びゅ

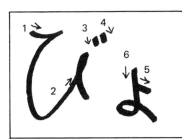

BYO

びょ	びょ	びょ	びょ	びょ	びょ

PYA

ぴゃ	ぴゃ	ぴゃ	ぴゃ	ぴゃ	ぴゃ

First, **TRACE** each character several times, paying strict attention to stroke order and direction. Then carefully draw the character in the blank squares. Take your time. Develop good habits NOW.

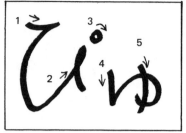

PYU

ぴゅ	ぴゅ	ぴゅ	ぴゅ	ぴゅ	ぴゅ

PYO

ぴょ	ぴょ	ぴょ	ぴょ	ぴょ	ぴょ

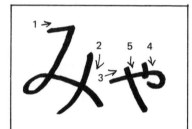

MYA

みゃ	みゃ	みゃ	みゃ	みゃ	みゃ

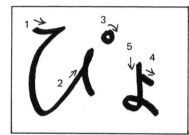

MYU

みゅ	みゅ	みゅ	みゅ	みゅ	みゅ

MYO

みょ	みょ	みょ	みょ	みょ	みょ

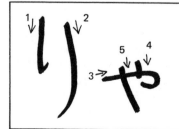

RYA

りゃ	りゃ	りゃ	りゃ	りゃ	りゃ

First, **TRACE** each character several times, paying strict attention to stroke order and direction.
Then carefully draw the character in the blank squares. Take your time. Develop good habits NOW.

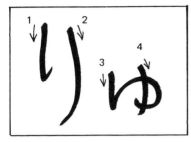

RYU

りゅ	りゅ	りゅ	りゅ	りゅ	りゅ

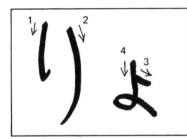

RYO

りょ	りょ	りょ	りょ	りょ	りょ

WRITING WORDS

If you can write all of the *HIRAGANA* characters, along with their voiced and bilabialized counterparts and combination characters, you have only a short way to go before you can read and write words, phrases, and sentences.

This section will teach you how double consonants and long vowels are made, and give you some practice at writing words. Words in this section were selected for writing practice only, not for vocabulary study. We advise that you NOT waste time looking up their meanings.

DOUBLE CONSONANTS

There are certain consonant sounds in the Japanese sound system that may be doubled, specifically /K/, /S/ (including /SH/), /T/ (including /CH/), and /P/. Note that only voiceless consonants may be doubled.

In each case the double consonant is represented in *HIRAGANA* by a small *TSU* (つ) placed immediately BEFORE the consonant sound to be doubled, as in the examples below.

HAKKIRI

HA	K	KI	RI

はっきり

MASSUGU

MA	S	SU	GU

まっすぐ

NESSHIN

NE	S	SHI	N

ねっしん

MATTAKU

MA	T	TA	KU

まったく

KETCHIN

KE	T	CHI	N

けっちん

IPPIKI

I	P	PI	KI

いっぴき

Notice that the *TSU* (つ) character is smaller than it would normally be written. Compare the following pairs:

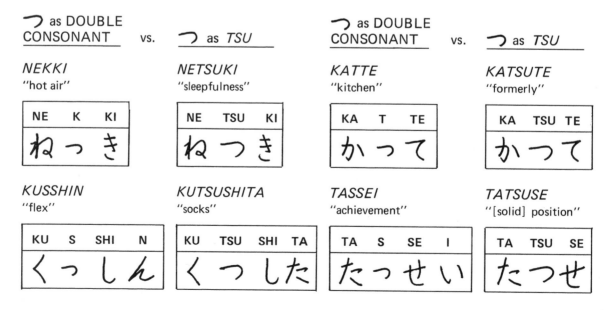

つ as DOUBLE CONSONANT   vs.   つ as *TSU*

NEKKI
"hot air"

NE	K	KI

ねっき

NETSUKI
"sleepfulness"

NE	TSU	KI

ねつき

つ as DOUBLE CONSONANT   vs.   つ as *TSU*

KATTE
"kitchen"

KA	T	TE

かって

KATSUTE
"formerly"

KA	TSU	TE

かつて

KUSSHIN
"flex"

KU	S	SHI	N

くっしん

KUTSUSHITA
"socks"

KU	TSU	SHI	TA

くつした

TASSEI
"achievement"

TA	S	SE	I

たっせい

TATSUSE
"[solid] position"

TA	TSU	SE

たつせ

Practice writing the following words that have double consonants. First, **TRACE** the *HIRAGANA* characters as shown, being careful to follow correct stroke order and direction as learned previously. Then write the words, character for character, in the blank spaces. These words were selected for writing practice only. We advise that you NOT waste time looking up their meanings.)

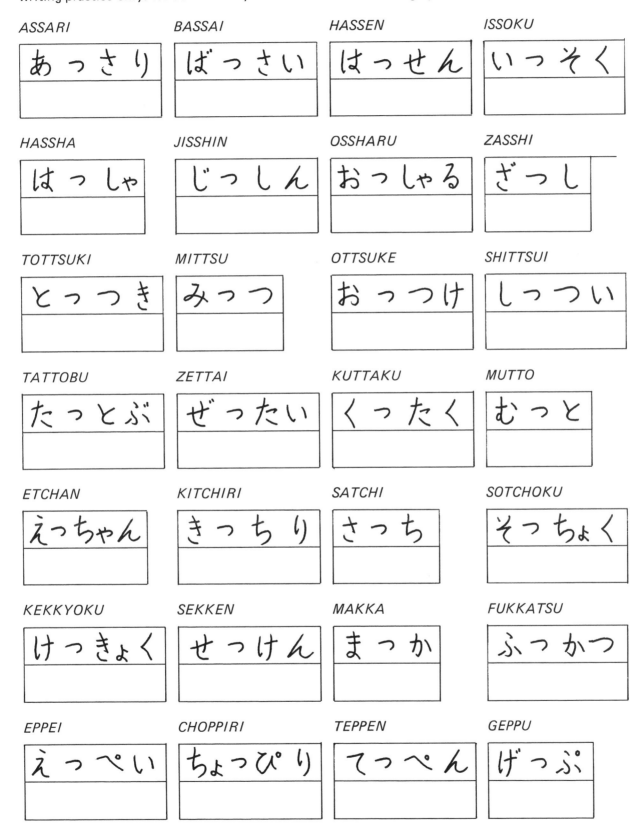

ASSARI	BASSAI	HASSEN	ISSOKU
あっさり	ばっさい	はっせん	いっそく
HASSHA	JISSHIN	OSSHARU	ZASSHI
はっしゃ	じっしん	おっしゃる	ざっし
TOTTSUKI	MITTSU	OTTSUKE	SHITTSUI
とっつき	みっつ	おっつけ	しっつい
TATTOBU	ZETTAI	KUTTAKU	MUTTO
たっとぶ	ぜったい	くったく	むっと
ETCHAN	KITCHIRI	SATCHI	SOTCHOKU
えっちゃん	きっちり	さっち	そっちょく
KEKKYOKU	SEKKEN	MAKKA	FUKKATSU
けっきょく	せっけん	まっか	ふっかつ
EPPEI	CHOPPIRI	TEPPEN	GEPPU
えっぺい	ちょっぴり	てっぺん	げっぶ

NOTE: Don't be confused when you see words that are romanized with double N, such as *ZANNEN, KONNICHI, MINNA,* etc. These are not treated as double consonants in *HIRAGANA,* since the first N is represented by the character ん , as follows:

ZANNEN

ZA	N	NE	N
ざ	ん	ね	ん

KONNICHI

KO	N	NI	CHI
こ	ん	に	ち

MINNA

MI	N	NA
み	ん	な

The character for *TSU* (つ) is NEVER used to double the consonant N.

LONG VOWELS

Long vowels are usually represented in *RŌMAJI* by a vowel with a line over it, as in *OKĀSAN, SENSHŪ, ONĒSAN, ŌSAKA.* The vowel I (and in some other forms of romanization, A, O, E, and U as well, may be romanized by repeating the vowel, as in *ONIISAN* and *CHIISAI.*

In *HIRAGANA* long vowels are usually represented by placing あ *(A),* い *(I),* う *(U),* え *(E),* or お *(O)* immediately after the character that has the corresponding vowel sound. In other words, as follows:

OKĀSAN

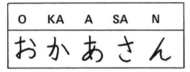

O	KA	A	SA	N

ONIISAN

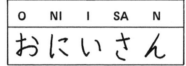

O	NI	I	SA	N

SENSHŪ

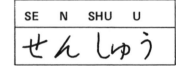

SE	N	SHU	U

ONĒSAN

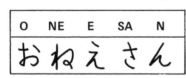

O	NE	E	SA	N

ŌSAKA

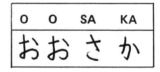

O	O	SA	KA

The exception to this rule is that the vowel O is often elongated by use of the character う *(U),* instead of お *(O).* Ordinarily, お is used to elongate an O that BEGINS a word, as in *ŌSAKA* (お おさか) and *ŌKII* (おおきい). When the long O is in the MIDDLE of a word or at the END of a word, the character う is more often used, as in

GAKKŌ

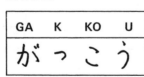

GA	K	KO	U

RYŌSHIN

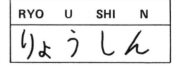

RYO	U	SHI	N

Rare exceptions to this rule should be memorized as you come across them. (Appendix B includes a brief list of common exceptions.)

Now practice writing the following words that have long vowels. First, **TRACE** the *HIRAGANA*, then write each word, character for character, in the space provided. Always be careful to follow the appropriate stroke order as learned previously.

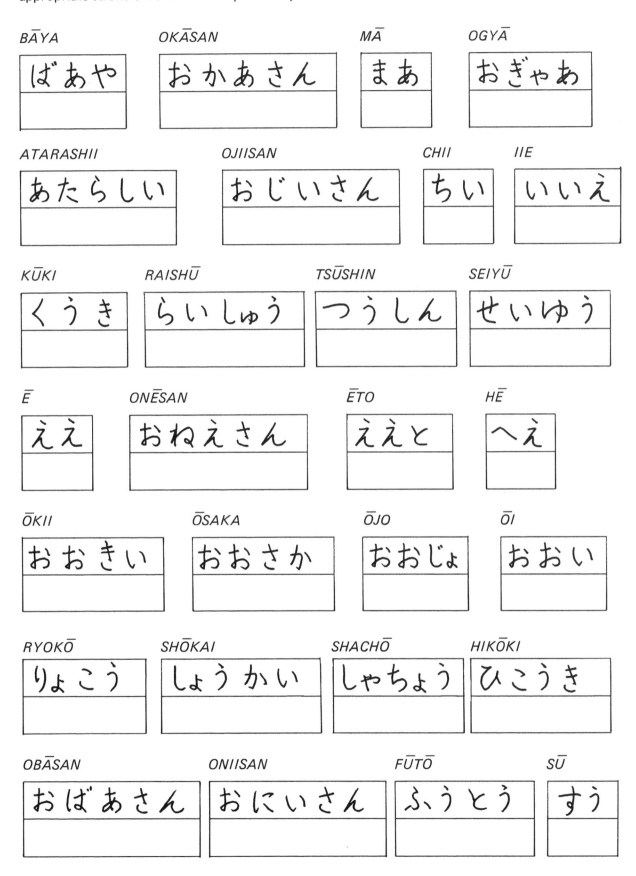

BĀYA

ばあや

OKĀSAN

おかあさん

MĀ

まあ

OGYĀ

おぎゃあ

ATARASHII

あたらしい

OJIISAN

おじいさん

CHII

ちい

IIE

いいえ

KŪKI

くうき

RAISHŪ

らいしゅう

TSŪSHIN

つうしん

SEIYŪ

せいゆう

Ē

ええ

ONĒSAN

おねえさん

ĒTO

ええと

HĒ

へえ

ŌKII

おおきい

ŌSAKA

おおさか

ŌJO

おおじょ

ŌI

おおい

RYOKŌ

りょこう

SHŌKAI

しょうかい

SHACHŌ

しゃちょう

HIKŌKI

ひこうき

OBĀSAN

おばあさん

ONIISAN

おにいさん

FŪTŌ

ふうとう

SŪ

すう

WRITING SENTENCES

PARTICLES

Other than the rules and guidelines given heretofore, there are few things to remember when writing sentences in *KANA*. There are, however, a couple of exceptions in the writing of particles.

A.   The topic particle *WA* is written NOT with the character わ , but with the character は *(HA)*, This is the ONLY time that は is not pronounced HA, and it is the ONLY time that the syllable *WA* is not written with わ . Note that the *WA* in *DEWA MATA, DEWA ARIMASEN,* and *DEWA ARIMASEN DESHITA* is related to the particle *WA* and is included in this rule.

Practice writing the following short sentences by first tracing the characters as given, then writing them in the spaces provided.

   KORE WA HON DEWA ARIMASEN.

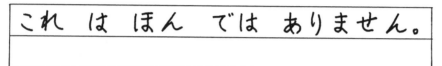

   これ は ほん では ありません。

   KARE WA GAKUSEI DEWA ARIMASEN DESHITA.

   かれ は がくせい では ありません でした。

B.   The direction particle *E* is written NOT with the character え , but with the character へ *(HE)*. This is the ONLY time that へ is not pronounced HE, and it is the ONLY time that the syllable *E* is not written with the character え .

Practice writing the following short sentences by first tracing the characters as given, then writing the characters in the spaces provided.

WATAKUSHI WA HON'YA E IKIMASU.

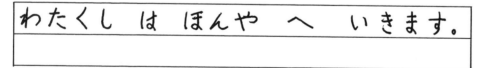

わたくし は ほんや へ いきます。

KANOJO WA YŪBINKYOKU E IKIMASHITA.

かのじょ は ゆうびんきょく へ いきました。

C. The direct object particle *O* is written with the character を . This is the only use for the character を . Any other time that the syllable *O* occurs (as in *ONAMAE, EGAO, KIOKU,* etc.), it is written with the character お .

Practice writing the following short sentences by first tracing the characters as given, then writing the characters in the spaces provided.

TOSHIO-SAN WA HON O KAIMASHITA.

としおさん は ほん を かいました。

OTŌSAN WA ŌKII KURUMA O MOTTE IMASU.

おとうさん は おおきい くるま を もって います。

SPACES

In ordinary Japanese reading material, when both *KANA* and *KANJI* are used, there are few—if any— spaces placed between words. However, when *KANA* is used exclusively, or when few *KANJI* are used, spaces are provided to make it easier to read and understand the meaning.

Notice the visual differences in the two versions of the following sentence.

WATAKUSHI WA YŪSHOKU O TABETE, HEYA NI ITTE, TEGAMI O KAKIMASHITA.

a) わたくし は ゆうしょく を たべて、へや に
いって、てがみ を かきました。

b) 私 は 夕食 を 食べて、部屋 に 行って、手紙 を 書
きました。

In version a), if there were no spaces to separate the words, it would be difficult to understand. In version b), however, the function of the spaces is performed by the *KANJI* characters, and so no spaces are really needed.

You should be aware that the Japanese often omit the space between a word and the particle that follows it, as well as spaces between the words of a verb phrase, as in the following example.

WATAKUSHI WA YŪSHOKU O TABETE, O-MISE NI ITTE KIMASHITA.

わたくしは ゆうしょくを たべて、おみせに
いってきました。

PUNCTUATION AND MISCELLANY

There are few rules of punctuation in Japanese, and there is a great deal of flexibility in their use.

The major marks of punctuation are as follows:

A. *KUTEN*   (period; also called *MARU,* meaning "circle")

This is used, as in English, to mark the end of a sentence. It also may mark the end of a question or an exclamatory sentence, after particles *KA* and *YO.* In casual writing, it has become common for the English question mark (?) and exclamation point (!) to be used instead, but it is still most common for the *KUTEN* to be used alone after the particle.

B. *TŌTEN*   (comma; literally, "reading point")

Rules for the use of *TŌTEN* are much less rigid than English rules for using commas, to the point that their use is almost arbitrary. They may be placed wherever a natural break in the sentence would occur—always AFTER a particle or conjunction, rather than before one.

C. *KAKKO*   (quotation marks)

Used much as in English, these are placed to the upper left and lower right of the first and last characters, respectively, of the word or words quoted in horizontal writing, but to the upper right and lower left of words quoted in vertical writing. (See examples in Practice and Self-Test Section.) It is also possible to make double quotations, as shown at left, although these are rarely used in Japanese.

D.   OTHER MARKS   The Japanese find use for brackets [ ] , ⟨ ⟩ and parentheses ( ) in situations similar to those for which they would be used in English. There is no strictly Japanese counterpart for these in current use.

Although hyphens (-) may be used when writing in *RŌMAJI,* they are never used when writing in Japanese script. However, occasionally a dash (—) may be used to indicate an interruption in thought, a long pause, or in place of a colon. Colons and semi-colons are not used with Japanese script.

Examples of these miscellaneous marks may be seen in the Practice and Self-Test Section.

UNDERLINING / PARAGRAPHS / LINE BREAKS

To place visual emphasis on or call attention to a word or words, the Japanese may underline them as in English, except that in vertical writing the line is drawn to the right of the characters.   (See examples in Practice and Self-Test Section.)

Paragraphs are indicated by an indentation, as in English. The indentation for Japanese script is usually the size of one character. Since Japanese characters represent syllables, the breaking of a word (at the end of a line, for example) may be done between any two characters, even between the two elements of a combination character. Lines may, therefore, be kept fairly uniform in length. There are no hyphens to indicate when a word has been broken at the end of a line, just as there may be no spaces between words. Once you become accustomed to reading without these English-style cues, they are not particularly missed.

VERTICAL WRITING

Shown below are two samples of *HIRAGANA* written vertically, one in machine-made characters and the other handwritten. Take careful note of the spacing and positioning of the characters, particularly the double consonant symbols (*) and combination characters (lined). Also notice how the quotation marks and other punctuation are arranged.

ひなたちは　かえってきた　ひばりに　いいました。
「おかあさん。　たいへん　です。　あした　おひゃくしょうさんが、　むぎかりに　くるそうですよ。」
ひばりは　こたえました。
「だいじょうぶですよ。　けっして　しんぱい　いりません。」

KANA REPETITION SYMBOLS

You should be aware of two symbols of repetition that are used by the Japanese, particularly in vertical writing. The first (example A, below) repeats only one *KANA* character; the second (example B) is used to repeat two or more characters. Symbol B is used ONLY in vertical writing. In words where a voiceless character or characters is repeated VOICED, the usual *NIGORI* symbol is used with the repetition symbol.

These symbols are not as commonly used today as formerly, but you will still see them from time to time as you practice reading Japanese.

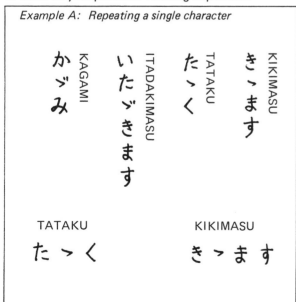

Example A: Repeating a single character

KIKIMASU きゝます
TATAKU たゝく
ITADAKIMASU いたゞきます
KAGAMI かゞみ

TATAKU たゝく
KIKIMASU きゝます

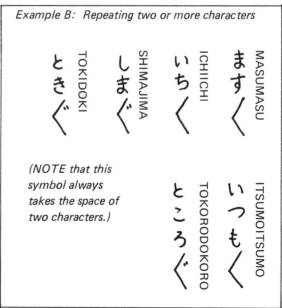

Example B: Repeating two or more characters

MASUMASU ますく
ICHIICHI いちく
SHIMAJIMA しまぐ
TOKIDOKI ときぐ
ITSUMOITSUMO いつもく
TOKORODOKORO ところぐ

(NOTE that this symbol always takes the space of two characters.)

PRACTICE & SELF-TEST

On the following pages are exercises to help you practice reading and writing in *HIRAGANA.*

Follow the instructions carefully. Some of the exercises require that you TRACE, COPY, and then ROMANIZE sentences given for you in *HIRAGANA.* Other exercises require that you write in *HIRAGANA* sentences that are presented in *RŌMAJI.*

In some exercises the *HIRAGANA* is presented in machine-made characters; in others it is hand-written. Some exercises are written horizontally, some are written vertically. Every effort has been made to give you experience in a variety of writing situations, as well as to expose you to some slightly different handwriting styles.

After you have finished each exercise, check your work carefully against the correct responses given in Appendix C in the back of this book. Translations of the sentences used in this section are given in Appendix D.

First, TRACE the following sentences, then COPY them, character for character, in the first blank space for each line. In the second blank space, ROMANIZE what you have written.

¹⁾ これ は なん です か。 ²⁾ それ は とけい

です。 ³⁾ あの ひと は だれ です か。 ⁴⁾ か

のじょ は たなかさん です。 ⁵⁾ しょくどう は あ

そこ です か。 ⁶⁾ おてあらい は どこ です か。

⁷⁾ かれ は せんせい ではありません。 ⁸⁾ あの

ひと は がいじん です か。 ⁹⁾ ゆうびんきょく

は むこう です。 ¹⁰⁾ わたくし は がくせい

でした。 ¹¹⁾ いりぐち は あそこ です ね。

Check your work against correct responses given in Appendix C.

First, TRACE the following sentences, then COPY them, character for character, in the first blank space for each line. In the second blank space, ROMANIZE what you have written.

1) なん です か。 2)としょかん は どこ に

あります か。 3)ぎんこう は むこう に

あります。 4)じゅうぎょういん は どこ に い

ます か。 5)じゅうぎょういん は あの へや

に います。 6)あの へや に は ごみ ば

こ が あります か。 7)きょうしつ に つく

え が ありません。 8)あの へや に だ

れ が いました か。 9)かれ は いません。

First, TRACE the following sentences, then COPY them, character for character, in the first blank space for each line. In the second blank space, ROMANIZE what you have written.

trace | りよく　いらっしゃいました。²⁾どこ　へ　いきま
copy |
rōmaji |

trace | す　か。³⁾けさ　がっこう　に　きました。⁴⁾き
copy |
rōmaji |

trace | のう　たなかさん　は　じむしょ　に　きません　で
copy |
rōmaji |

trace | した。⁵⁾しゃちょうさん　は　きょう　たくしい　で　かえ
copy |
rōmaji |

trace | りました。⁶⁾あなた　は　もう　かえります　か。
copy |
rōmaji |

trace | ⁷⁾かのじょ　は　なんで　とうきょう　に　いきました
copy |
rōmaji |

trace | か。⁸⁾わたくし　は　きのう　ゆうびんきょく　へ
copy |
rōmaji |

trace | いきません　でした。⁹⁾かれ　は　ともだち　です。
copy |
rōmaji |

Check your work against correct responses given in Appendix C.

First, TRACE the following sentences, then COPY them, character for character, in the first blank space for each line. In the second blank space, ROMANIZE what you have written.

¹⁾ あの ひと は にほんご を べんきょう して

いますか。 ²⁾ しゃちょうさん に もう いちど

でんわ を して ください。 ³⁾ かのじょ は しん

ぶん を よんで いません。 ⁴⁾ たなかさん は

くるま を ゆうびんきょく まで うんてん しま

した。 ⁵⁾ わたくし は ほんや へ いきました

けれども、 ほん を かいません でした。 ⁶⁾ きょ

う わたくし と たべて くださいません か。

Check your work against correct responses given in Appendix C.

First, TRACE the following sentences, then COPY them, character for character, in the first blank space for each line. In the second blank space, ROMANIZE what you have written.

1) あなた は なぜ きょうしつ に いきません

か。 2) あした まで でんわ しないで ください。

3) らいしゅう また くる こと が できます か。

4) こんばん いそがしい です から、いく こと

が できません。 5) おきゃくさま が すぐ きます

ので、まだ かえらないで ください。 6) おにい

さん は なぜ たべません でした か。 7) じゅ

ういちじ まで べんきょう しましょう、ね。

First, TRACE the following sentences, then COPY them, character for character, in the blank space to the right of each line. Then ROMANIZE them on the blank horizontal lines at the bottom.

trace	copy

1. どう いう いみ です か。 2. しつもん が あります か。

3. おはよう ございます。 4. おやすみ なさい。 5. ああ、そ

う です か。 6. では また。 7. わかります、でしょう。

8. さようなら。 9. いくら です か。 10. いちまんごせん にひ

ゃくじゅうどる です。 11. たかい です、ね。 12. いいえ、

やすい です よ。 13. おなまえ は なん です か。 14. た

なか と もうします。 15. はじめまして。 16. よろしく お

ねがい します。 17. どうも ありがとう ございます。 18. どう

いたしまして。 19. きゅうひゃくろくじゅうごえん です。

Romanize:

_____
_____
_____
_____
_____
_____
_____

Check your work against the correct responses in Appendix C.

First, TRACE the following sentences, then COPY them, character for character, in the blank space to the right of each line. Then ROMANIZE them on the blank horizontal lines at the bottom.

1.

trace copy trace copy trace copy trace copy trace copy trace copy trace copy trace copy

1. でぐち は どこ です か。
2. いりぐち は むこう です、
ね。
3. かれ は せんせい では ありません か。
4. わたくし の だいがく は とうきょう に あります。
5. あなた の つくえ は どれ です か。
6. ざんねん です、ね。
7. じむしょ に は ごみばこ も とけい も あります。
8. どの へや が かれ の です か。
9. きょうしつ に は、せんせい も がくせい も います。
10. しゃちょうさん と じゅうぎょういん は いま その へや に います か。
11. あなた の くるま は むこう に ありません でした。

Romanize:

_____

_____

_____

_____

_____

_____

Check your work against the correct responses in Appendix C.

First, TRACE the following sentences, then COPY them, character for character, in the blank space to the right of each line. Then ROMANIZE them on the blank horizontal lines at the bottom.

1.

trace	copy	trace	copy	trace	copy	trace	copy	trace	copy	trace	copy	trace	copy	trace	copy	trace	copy

とは いま へや で てがみ を よんで います。

た。 11. おとうと は おおさか で はたらいて います か。 12. いもう

10. さくばん だいがく の でぐち で たなかさん と まって いまし

した。 9. かれ は じゅうじ じゅうごふん まえ に かえりました。

あさん と おねえさん は いっしょ に しょくどう で たべて いま

ま でした。 6. ちょっと まって ください。 7. いって きます。 8. おか

おねえさん と いっしょ に ちかてつ で かえります。 5. ごちそうさ

しゅう ゆうびんきょく へ いきました か。 4. らいしゅう まいにち

いらっしゃいませ。 2. こんど は いっしょ に いきましょう。 3. せん

Romanize:

_____

_____

_____

_____

_____

_____

Check your work against the correct responses in Appendix C.

First, TRACE the following sentences, then COPY them, character for character, in the blank space to the right of each line. Then ROMANIZE them on the blank horizontal lines at the bottom.

1.

trace	copy	trace	copy	trace	copy	trace	copy	trace	copy	trace	copy	trace	copy	trace	copy

1. おじゃま します。 2. おたんじょうび おめでとう ございます。 3. いつ

も どこ で きゅうけい を します か。 4. いちにちぢゅう べんきょ

う する こと が できません でした。 5. おかね が ありません の

で まだ ほん を かわないで ください。 6. みんな は にほんご が

できます か。 7. おとうさん は ことし にほん で りょこう を

して います。 8. あした の あさ、 がっこう で せんせい と はな

して くださいません か。 9. おなか が すいて います けれども、

まだ しょくじ が できません。 10. げつようび は きゅうじつ です

から、 わたくしたち は しごと へ いきません。

Romanize:

_____

_____

_____

_____

_____

_____

_____

Check your work against the correct responses in Appendix C.

First, COPY each line of the dialogue below onto the first blank space beneath it. In the second blank space ROMANIZE each line of dialogue, checking your work carefully with Appendix C.

たなか　「せんせい　は　きょうしつ　に　います　か。」

_____

_____

ほんだ　「いいえ、　じむしょ　に　います。」

_____

_____

たなか　「じむしょ　は　どこ　に　あります　か。」

_____

_____

ほんだ　「むこう　に　あります。」

_____

_____

たなか　「この　へん　に　は　ごみばこ　が　あります　か。」

_____

_____

ほんだ　「ごみばこ　は　あの　へや　に　あります。」

_____

_____

たなか　「おてあらい　も　あります　か。」

_____

_____

ほんだ　「いいえ、　ありません。　としょかん　に　あります。」

_____

_____

たなか　「どうも　ありがとう　ございます。」

_____

_____

First, COPY each line of the dialogue below onto the blank space to the right of it. Then write the dialogue in ROMAJI on the lines at the bottom of the page. Check your work with Appendix C.

copy *copy* *copy* *copy* *copy* *copy* *copy* *copy*

さとう 「おともだち に でんわ を しましょう か。」

あき 「きょう いません から、まだ しないで ください。」

さとう 「はい、わかりました。では、としょかん へ いきましょう か。」

あき 「すみません が、きょう いそいで います ので、できません。ごめん なさい、ね。」

さとう 「いい です よ。あした は どう です か。」

あき 「はい、あした は けっこう です よ。」

Romanize:

_____

_____

_____

_____

_____

_____

_____

_____

Write the following sentences in *HIRAGANA* in the spaces provided. Check your work carefully against the correct responses given in Appendix C.

1. *SORE WA ANATA NO HON DESU KA?*

    _____

2. *KARE WA SENSEI DEWA ARIMASEN DESHITA.*

    _____

3. *TOSHOKAN WA MUKŌ DESU.*

    _____

4. *ANATA WA GAKUSEI DEWA ARIMASEN KA?*

    _____

5. *YŪBINKYOKU WA DORE DESU KA?*

    _____

6. *SORE WA KANOJO NO JISHO DESU, NE?*

    _____

7. *ANO HITO NO TSUKUE WA ASOKO DESU.*

    _____

8. *TANAKA-SAN NO TOKEI WA TAKAI, DESHŌ?*

    _____

9. *ANO HITOBITO WA DAIGAKUSEI DESHITA.*

    _____

10. *MUKŌ NO HITO WA SHACHŌ-SAN DESU, NE?*

    _____

11. *HON'YA-SAN WA GAIJIN DESU.*

    _____

12. *WATAKUSHI-TACHI WA NIHONJIN DEWA ARIMASEN.*

    _____

Write the following sentences in *HIRAGANA* in the spaces provided. Check your work carefully against the correct responses given in Appendix C.

1. *O-TOMODACHI WA IMA SHOKUDŌ NI IMASU.*

2. *O-TEARAI WA DOKO NI ARIMASU KA?*

3. *WATAKUSHI WA KURUMA GA ARIMASEN.*

4. *KANOJO WA SENSHŪ TŌKYŌ NI IMASHITA.*

5. *SEITO-TACHI WA KINŌ KYŌSHITSU NI IMASEN DESHITA.*

6. *ANO HEYA NI WA DARE GA IMASU KA?*

7. *KONO JITENSHA WA KARE NO DEWA ARIMASEN.*

8. *JŪGYŌIN MO SHACHŌ-SAN MO JIMUSHO NI IMASU.*

9. *GOMIBAKO MO O-TEARAI NI ARIMASU KA?*

10. *ANO HITOBITO WA KINŌ NO ASA YŪBINKYOKU NI IMASHITA.*

11. *SHOKUDŌ WA ASOKO NI ARIMASU, NE?*

12. *GINKŌ MO TOSHOKAN MO SOKO NI ARIMASU.*

Write the following sentences in *HIRAGANA* in the spaces provided. Check your work carefully against the correct responses given in Appendix C.

1. *ANATA WA KYŌ TOSHOKAN NI IKIMASU KA?*

2. *YŪBE SHOKUDŌ E IKIMASEN DESHITA.*

3. *SHACHŌ-SAN WA HIKŌKI DE TŌKYŌ E IKIMASHITA, DESHŌ?*

4. *ONĒSAN WA MAINICHI CHIKATETSU DE KAERIMASU.*

5. *SENGETSU MINNA WA DENSHA DE KIMASHITA.*

6. *RAINEN FUNE DE IKIMASHŌ.*

7. *ONIISAN TO ISSHO NI KIMASHITA, NE?*

8. *IMA WATAKUSHI WA JIKAN GA ARIMASEN.*

9. *IMŌTO-SAN WA MŌ KAERIMASHITA KA?*

10. *O-TOMODACHI WA HIKŌKI DE CHŪGOKU E KAERIMASHITA KA?*

11. *GO-SHUJIN WA SAKUBAN NO KAI NI IKIMASHITA KA?*

12. *TANAKA-SAN WA ASHITA SAPPORO E KAERIMASU.*

Write the following sentences in *HIRAGANA* in the spaces provided. Check your work carefully against the correct responses given in Appendix C.

1. *ANATA WA IMA NANI O SHITE IMASU KA?*

2. *KARE NO RYŌSHIN WA ŌSAKA NI SUNDE IMASU.*

3. *KANOJO WA HEYA DE TEGAMI O KAITE IMASU.*

4. *ONIISAN TO OTŌSAN WA ISSHO NI HASHITTE IMASHITA.*

5. *O-TOMODACHI TO MUKŌ NI SUWATTE KUDASAI.*

6. *MINNA WA MŌ UCHI E KAETTE IMASU.*

7. *SUKOSHI BENKYŌ SHITE KUDASAIMASEN KA?*

8. *TOSHOKAN E IKIMASU KEREDOMO, BENKYŌ SHIMASEN.*

9. *TANAKA-SAN WA KESA MUKŌ NI TATTE IMASHITA.*

10. *KANOJO-TACHI WA MADA KYŪKEI O SHITE IMASU.*

11. *ANO UTA O UTATTE KUDASAIMASU KA?*

12. *WATAKUSHI WA GINKŌ DE HATARAITE IMASEN DESHITA.*

Write the following sentences in *HIRAGANA* in the spaces provided. Check your work carefully against the correct responses given in Appendix C.

1. *ASHITA WA KYŪJITSU DESU KARA, YASUNDE KUDASAI.*

    ┌───┐
    │   │
    └───┘

2. *NIHONGO O HANASU KOTO GA DEKIMASU KA?*

    ┌───┐
    │   │
    └───┘

3. *BYŌKI DESU NODE, JIMUSHO E IKANAIDE KUDASAI.*

    ┌───┐
    │   │
    └───┘

4. *RAIGETSU NO KAI NI IKU KOTO GA DEKIMASEN KA?*

    ┌───┐
    │   │
    └───┘

5. *KANOJO WA UTAU KOTO GA DEKIMASEN.*

    ┌───┐
    │   │
    └───┘

6. *MŌ SUKOSHI MATSU KOTO GA DEKIMASU KA?*

    ┌───┐
    │   │
    └───┘

7. *TAKAI DESU NODE, KAWANAIDE KUDASAI.*

    ┌───┐
    │   │
    └───┘

8. *ANATA WA NAZE HANKAGAI E IKIMASEN DESHITA KA?*

    ┌───┐
    │   │
    └───┘

9. *JIKAN GA ARIMASEN KARA, MADA TABENAIDE KUDASAI.*

    ┌───┐
    │   │
    └───┘

10. *KYŌSHITSU DE TOMODACHI TO HANASANAIDE KUDASAI.*

    ┌───┐
    │   │
    └───┘

11. *KURUMA GA ARIMASEN KARA, DENSHA DE IKIMASU.*

    ┌───┐
    │   │
    └───┘

12. *EIGO GA DEKIMASEN NODE, NIHONGO DE HANASHITE IMASHITA.*

    ┌───┐
    │   │
    └───┘

KATAKANA NO GOJŪON

The chart below contains the "fifty sounds" (again, actually only 46 sounds) of the *KATAKANA* syllabary.

Note that these characters represent the same sounds as *HIRAGANA;* only the usage is different. *KATAKANA* is used primarily to write words and names of foreign origin. It is also used to place emphasis on or call attention to a word or phrase and is used liberally in advertising.

Begin here. ↓

ワ WA	ラ RA	ヤ YA	マ MA	ハ HA	ナ NA	タ TA	サ SA	カ KA	ア A
	リ RI		ミ MI	ヒ HI	ニ NI	チ CHI	シ SHI	キ KI	イ I
	ル RU	ユ YU	ム MU	フ FU	ヌ NU	ツ TSU	ス SU	ク KU	ウ U
	レ RE		メ ME	ヘ HE	ネ NE	テ TE	セ SE	ケ KE	エ E
ヲ (W)O	ロ RO	ヨ YO	モ MO	ホ HO	ノ NO	ト TO	ソ SO	コ KO	オ O
ン N'									

This chart is given in machine-made characters in Appendix A.

WRITING CHARACTERS

Review the information on page 5 about writing *KANA,* then proceed with the *KATAKANA* writing exercises that begin on page 54. As always, be careful to follow correct stroke order and stroke direction, as indicated by the numbers and arrows accompanying each demonstration character. Take your time. Use this opportunity to develop good writing habits and penmanship.

First, **TRACE** each character several times, paying strict attention to stroke order and direction. Then carefully draw the character in the blank squares. Take your time. Develop good habits NOW.

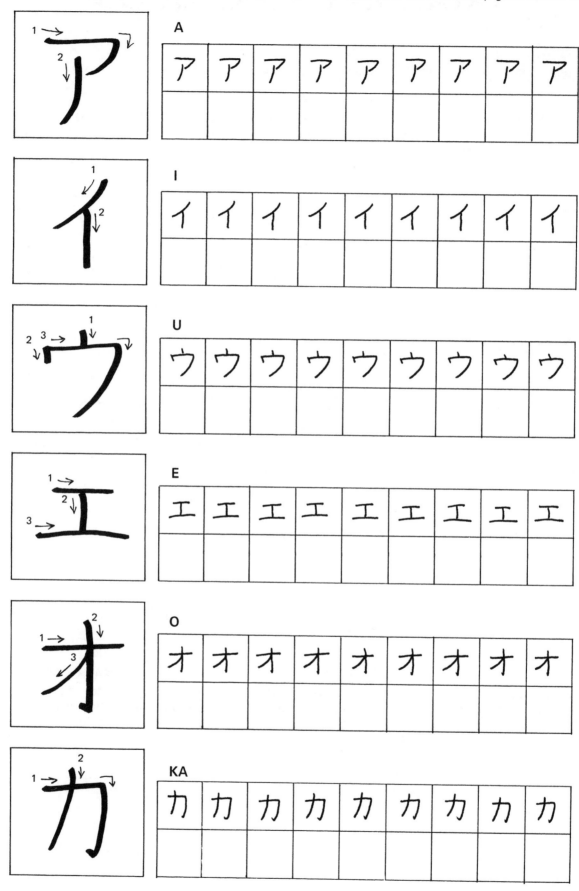

First, **TRACE** each character several times, paying strict attention to stroke order and direction. Then carefully draw the character in the blank squares. Take your time. Develop good habits NOW.

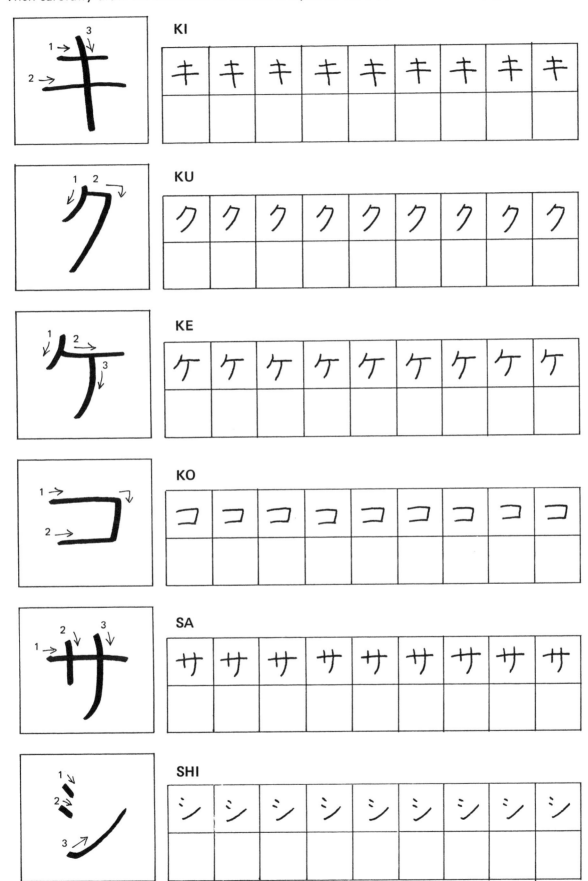

First, **TRACE** each character several times, paying strict attention to stroke order and direction.
Then carefully draw the character in the blank squares. Take your time. Develop good habits NOW.

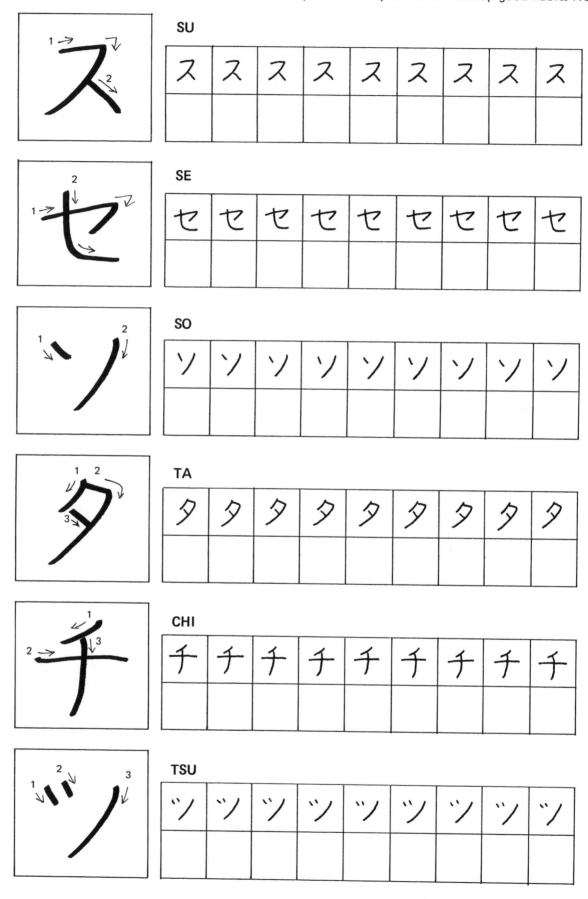

SU

SE

SO

TA

CHI

TSU

First, **TRACE** each character several times, paying strict attention to stroke order and direction.
Then carefully draw the character in the blank squares. Take your time. Develop good habits NOW.

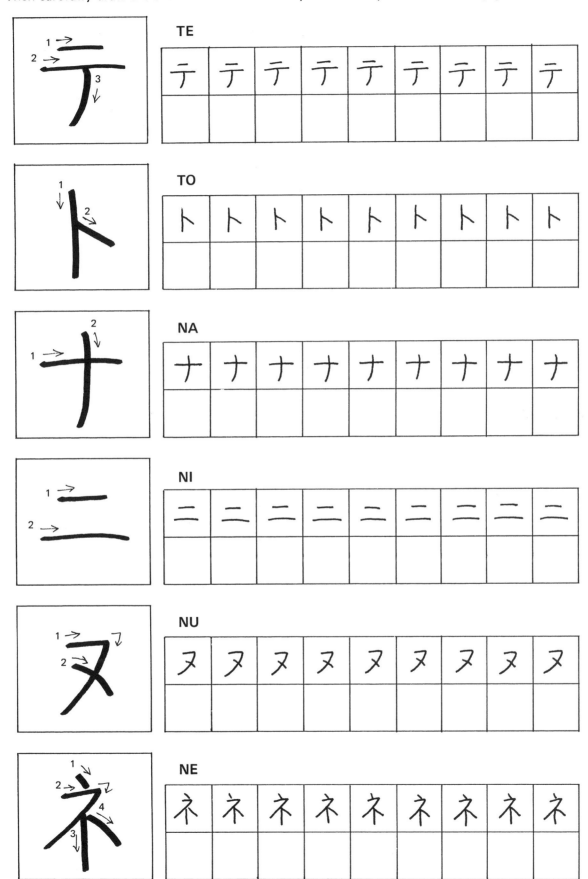

TE

TO

NA

NI

NU

NE

First, **TRACE** each character several times, paying strict attention to stroke order and direction.
Then carefully draw the character in the blank squares. Take your time. Develop good habits NOW.

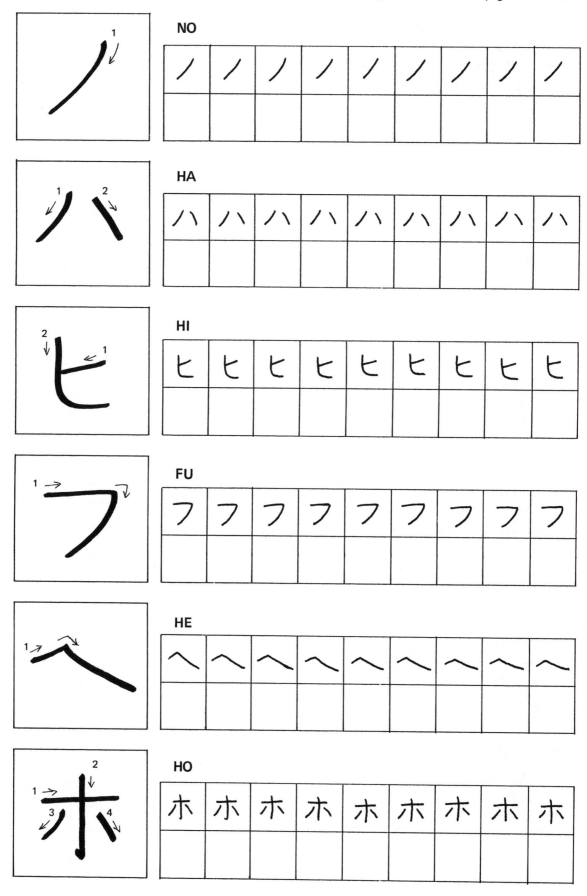

NO

HA

HI

FU

HE

HO

First, **TRACE** each character several times, paying strict attention to stroke order and direction. Then carefully draw the character in the blank squares. Take your time. Develop good habits NOW.

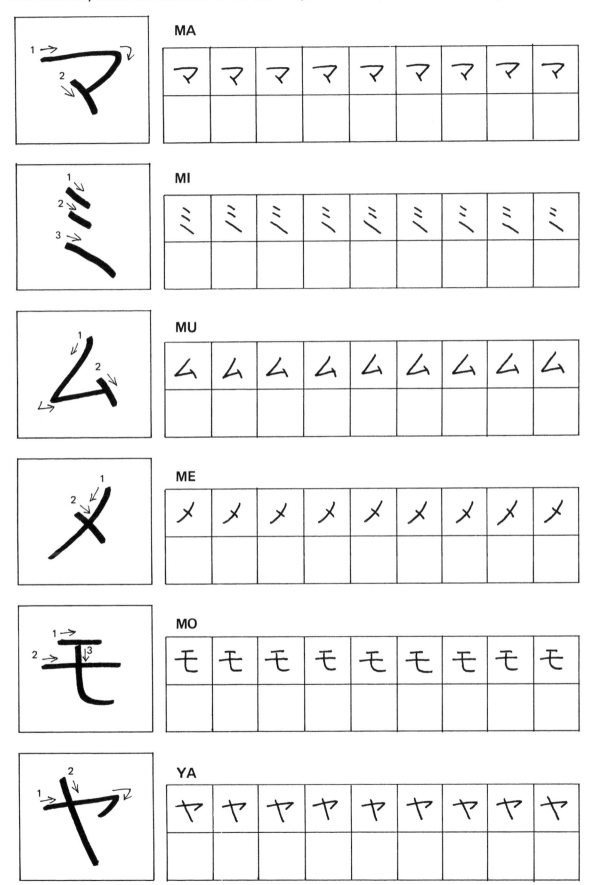

First, **TRACE** each character several times, paying strict attention to stroke order and direction. Then carefully draw the character in the blank squares. Take your time. Develop good habits NOW.

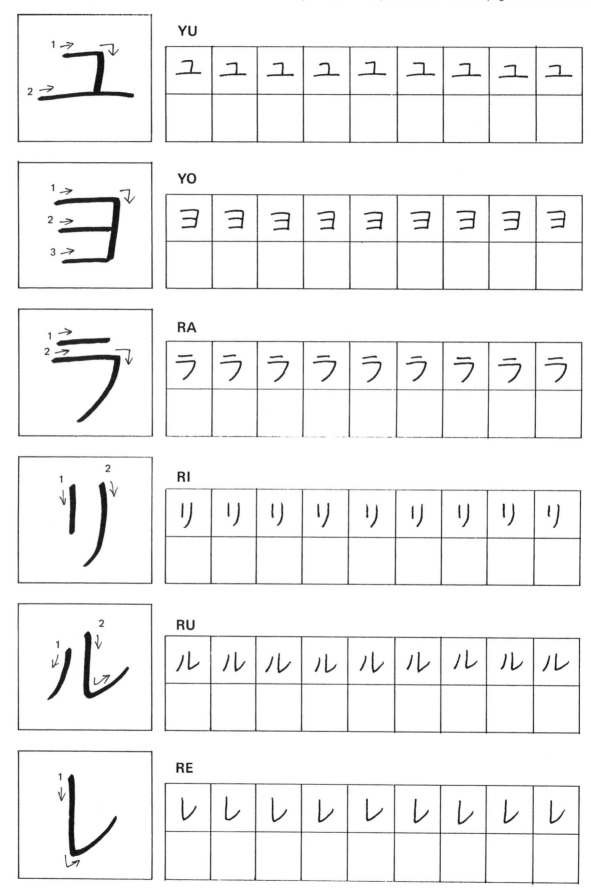

First, **TRACE** each character several times, paying strict attention to stroke order and direction. Then carefully draw the character in the blank squares. Take your time. Develop good habits NOW.

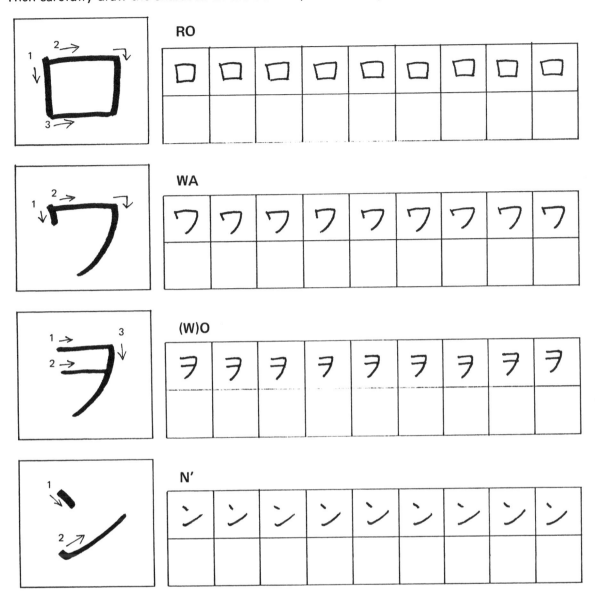

VOICED AND VOICELESS CONSONANTS

Now review the information on pages 14 and 15 regarding voiced and voiceless consonants and bilabials. All of the information given regarding *HIRAGANA* on those pages is true also for *KATAKANA.*

After you have reviewed that information, proceed with the exercises that begin on page 62 on writing these voiced and voiceless characters in *KATAKANA.* Don't rush. Take this opportunity to develop good writing habits and penmanship. Be careful to follow correct stroke order and stroke direction, as indicated by the numbers and arrows accompanying each demonstration character.

First, **TRACE** each character several times, paying strict attention to stroke order and direction.
Then carefully draw the character in the blank squares. Take your time. Develop good habits NOW.

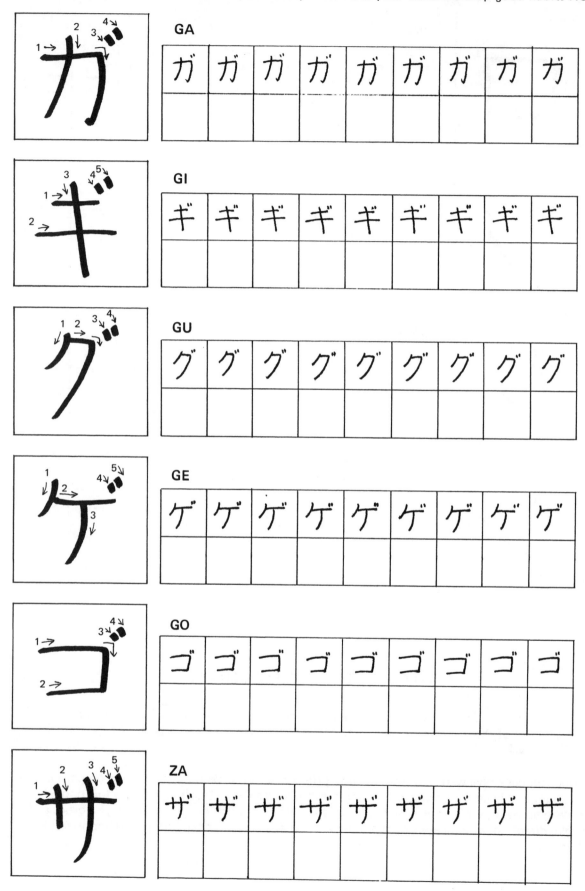

GA

ガ ガ ガ ガ ガ ガ ガ ガ ガ

GI

ギ ギ ギ ギ ギ ギ ギ ギ ギ

GU

グ グ グ グ グ グ グ グ グ

GE

ゲ ゲ ゲ ゲ ゲ ゲ ゲ ゲ ゲ

GO

ゴ ゴ ゴ ゴ ゴ ゴ ゴ ゴ ゴ

ZA

ザ ザ ザ ザ ザ ザ ザ ザ ザ

First, **TRACE** each character several times, paying strict attention to stroke order and direction. Then carefully draw the character in the blank squares. Take your time. Develop good habits NOW.

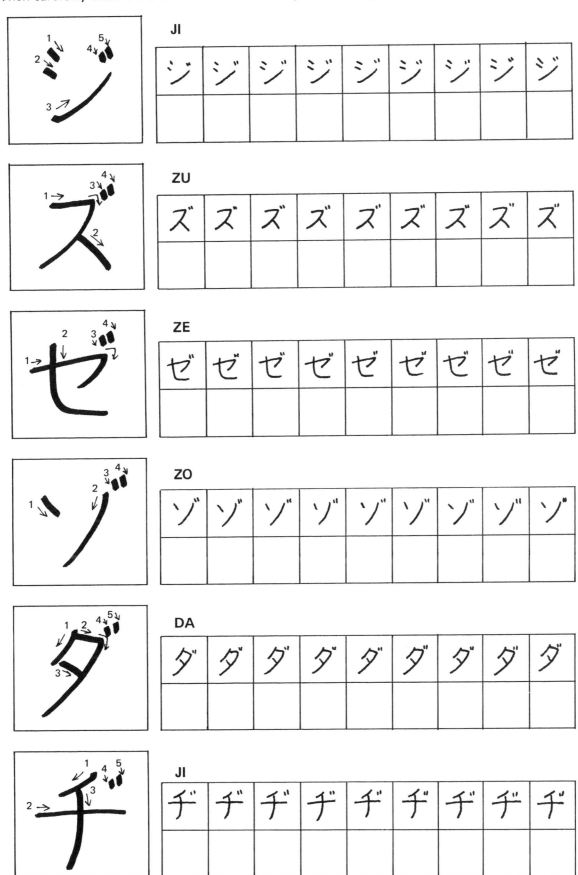

JI

ZU

ZE

ZO

DA

JI

First, **TRACE** each character several times, paying strict attention to stroke order and direction. Then carefully draw the character in the blank squares. Take your time. Develop good habits NOW.

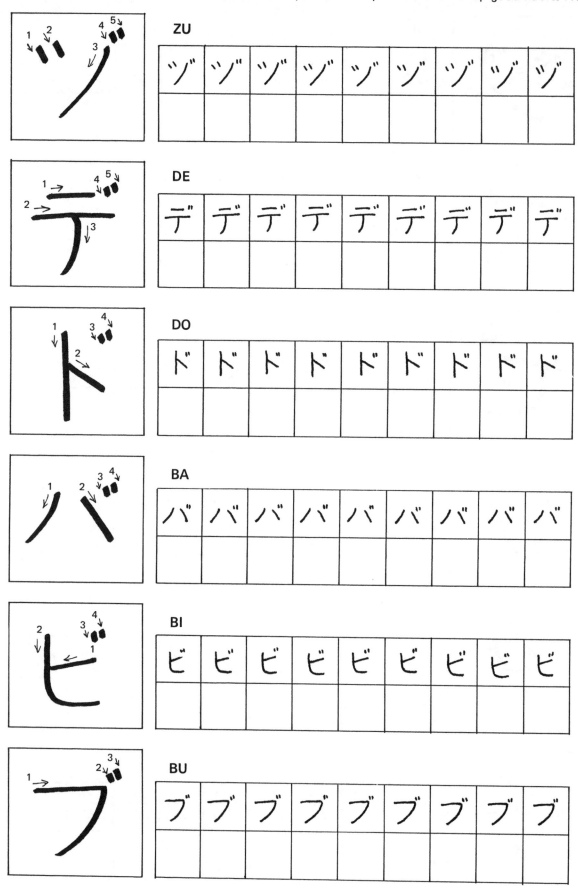

First, **TRACE** each character several times, paying strict attention to stroke order and direction. Then carefully draw the character in the blank squares. Take your time. Develop good habits NOW.

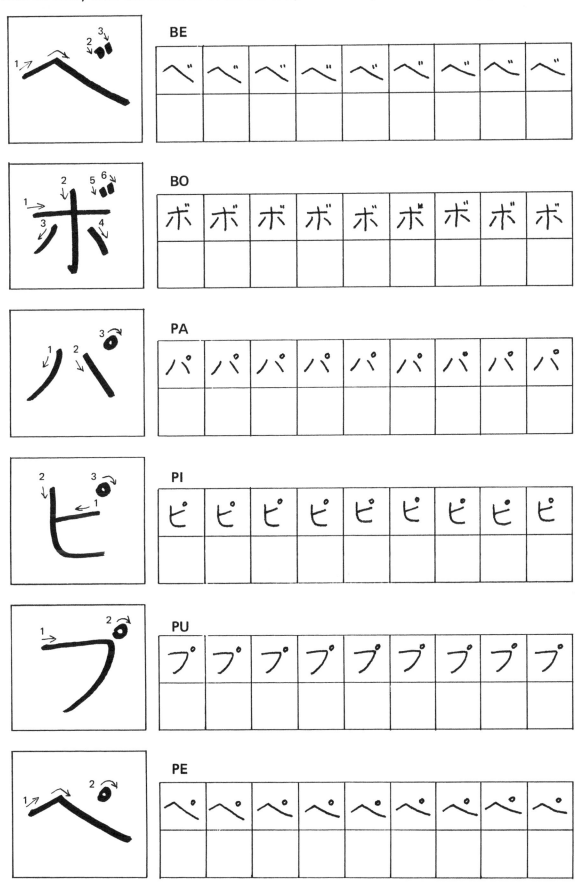

First, **TRACE** the character several times, paying strict attention to stroke order and direction. Then carefully draw the character in the blank squares. Take your time. Develop good habits NOW.

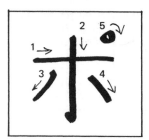

PO

ポ	ポ	ポ	ポ	ポ	ポ	ポ	ポ	ポ

COMBINATION CHARACTERS

Review the information on pages 20 and 21. All of the information given regarding *HIRAGANA* on those pages is true also for *KATAKANA*.

After you have reviewed that information carefully, proceed with the following exercises on writing these combination characters in *KATAKANA*. First, **TRACE** each character several times, paying strict attention to stroke order and direction. Then carefully draw the character in the blank squares. Take your time. Use this opportunity to develop good writing habits and penmanship.

First, **TRACE** each character several times, paying strict attention to stroke order and direction. Then carefully draw the character in the blank squares. Take your time. Develop good habits NOW.

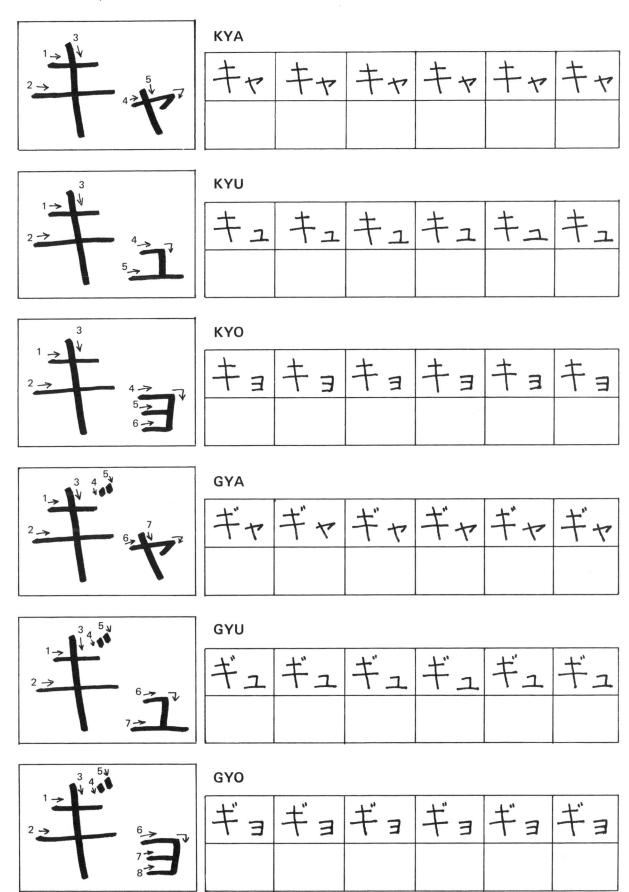

First, **TRACE** each character several times, paying strict attention to stroke order and direction. Then carefully draw the character in the blank squares. Take your time. Develop good habits NOW.

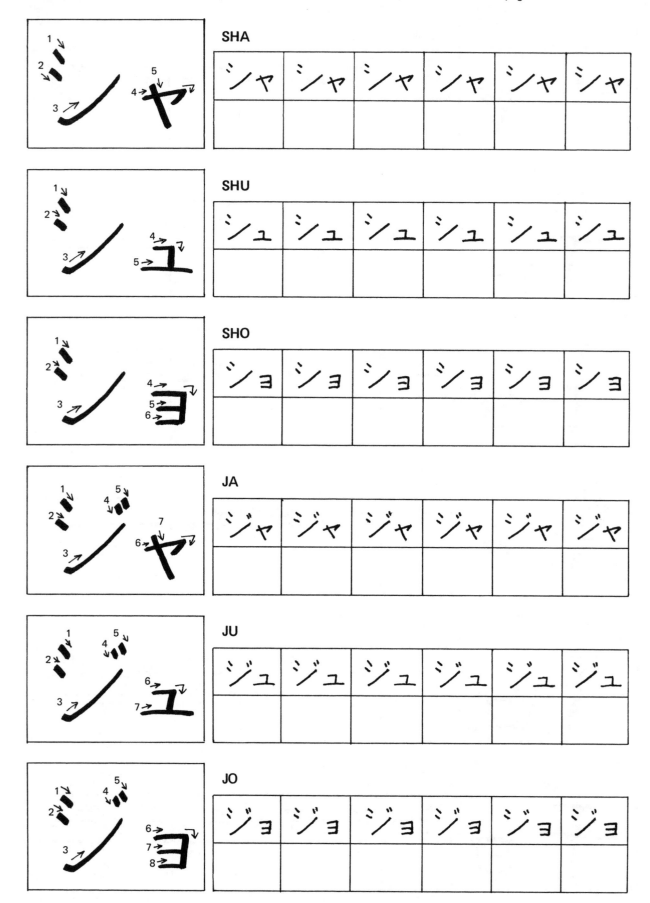

SHA

SHU

SHO

JA

JU

JO

First, **TRACE** each character several times, paying strict attention to stroke order and direction. Then carefully draw the character in the blank squares. Take your time. Develop good habits NOW.

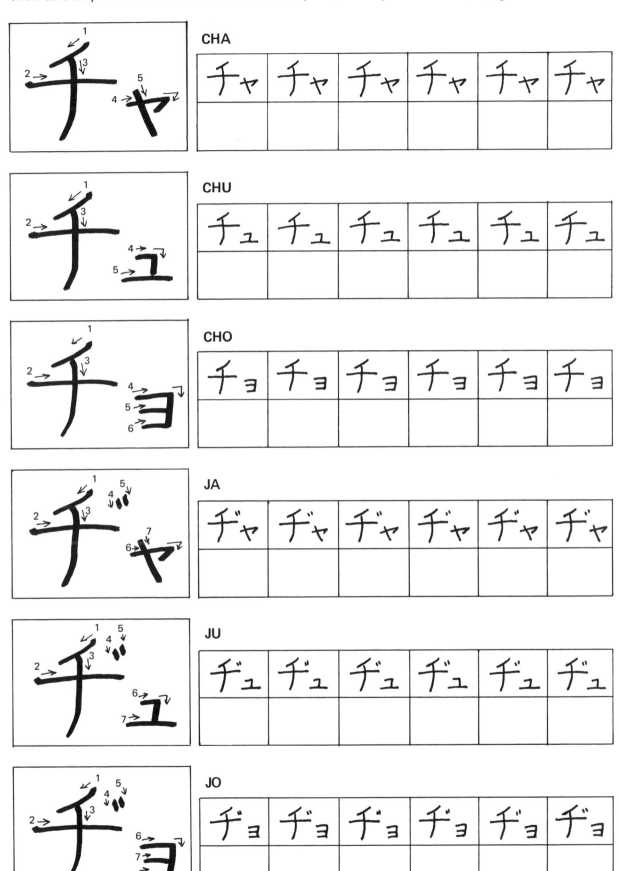

First, **TRACE** each character several times, paying strict attention to stroke order and direction. Then carefully draw the character in the blank squares. Take your time. Develop good habits NOW.

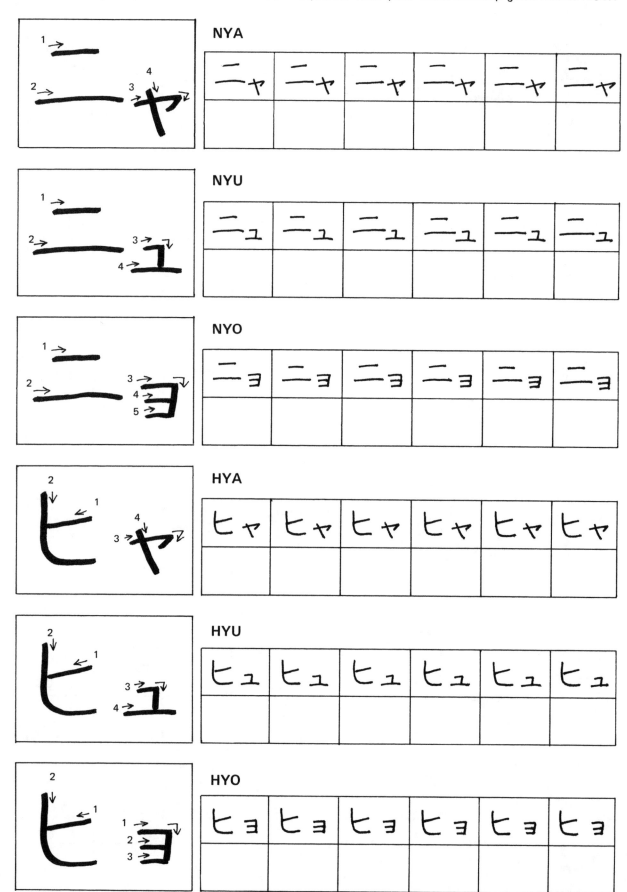

First, **TRACE** each character several times, paying strict attention to stroke order and direction. Then carefully draw the character in the blank squares. Take your time. Develop good habits NOW.

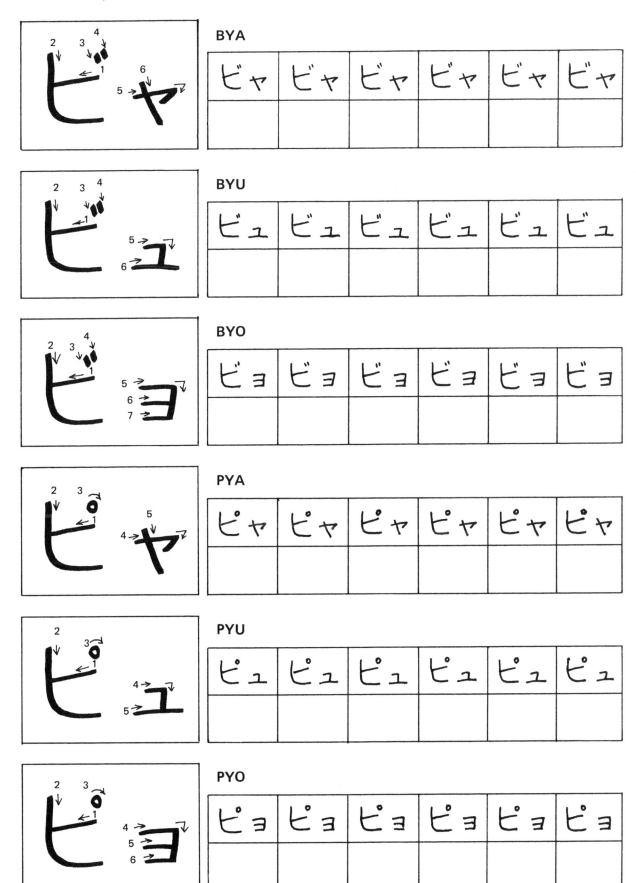

BYA

BYU

BYO

PYA

PYU

PYO

First, **TRACE** each character several times, paying strict attention to stroke order and direction. Then carefully draw the character in the blank squares. Take your time. Develop good habits NOW.

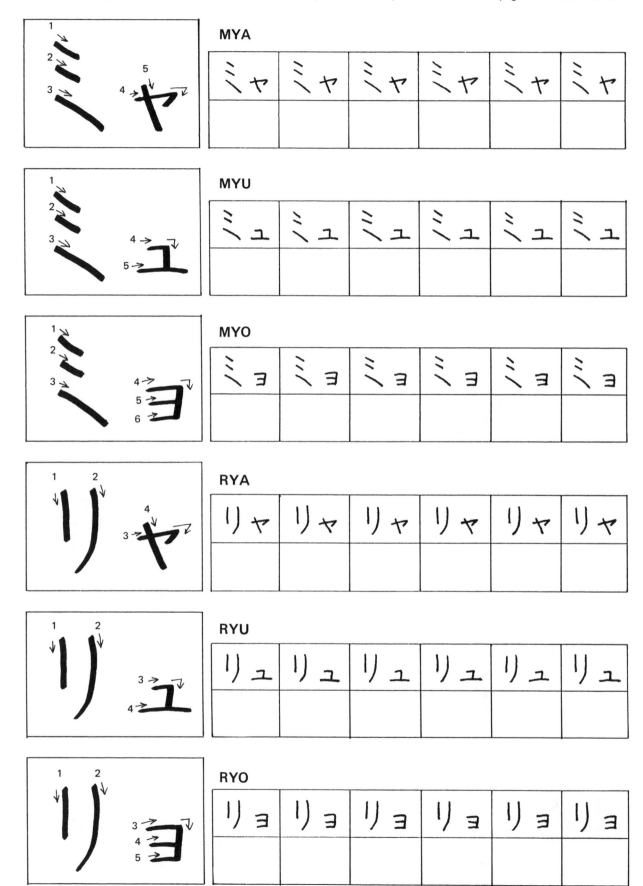

MYA

MYU

MYO

RYA

RYU

RYO

WRITING WORDS

Most of the information given in regard to the use of *HIRAGANA* in writing words is true also for *KATAKANA*. This section will teach you the few minor differences, plus some special instructions to help you learn to use *KATAKANA* quickly and correctly.

Before you continue with this section, REVIEW PAGES 28 - 31 of the section on writing words in *HIRAGANA*. Then come back to this page and proceed with the exercises that follow.

DOUBLE CONSONANTS

Rules for double consonants are exactly the same in *KATAKANA* as in *HIRAGANA*. Practice writing the examples shown below (first, TRACE, then copy), paying careful attention to the use of the character *TSU (ッ)*.

SUNAKKU ("snack shop")

スナック

ROKETTO ("rocket")

ロケット

HOTTO DOGGU ("hot dog")

ホット　ドッグ

Notice that voiced consonants (as in *HOTTO DOGGU*) may be doubled in *KATAKANA;* whereas, there are no doubled voiced consonants in the Japanese language, and therefore no doubled voiced consonants in *HIRAGANA*.

As with *HIRAGANA,* of course, the double N is represented by use of the single-consonant character *N' (ン)*.

TONNERU ("tunnel")

トンネル

INNINGU ("inning")

インニング

LONG VOWELS

One major difference between *HIRAGANA* and *KATAKANA* usage is in the representation of long vowels. If you are writing a JAPANESE WORD in *KATAKANA*, the exact same rules apply as when writing in *HIRAGANA;* however, if you are writing a NON-JAPANESE WORD in *KATAKANA*, any vowel may be elongated by writing a dash (—) after it. Note the differences in the the Japanese and non-Japanese examples below as you TRACE and then copy each one in the spaces provided.

JAPANESE WORDS	NON-JAPANESE WORDS
OKĀSAN ("mother")	*APĀTO* ("apartment")
オカアサン	アパート
ONIISAN ("older brother")	*TAKUSHII* ("taxi")
オニイサン	タクシー
KŪKI ("air")	*JŪSU* ("juice,")
クウキ	ジュース
ONĒSAN ("older sister")	*SĒRU* ("sale")
オネエサン	セール
BYŌKI ("sick")	*KŌHII* ("coffee")
ビョウキ	コーヒー
ŌSAKA ("Osaka")	*ŌTOMIIRU* ("oatmeal")
オオサカ	オートミール

When writing vertically in *KATAKANA*, you should write the dash vertically also:

SUKII
("ski")

SŪPĀ
("super-
market")

IMĒJI
("image")

MIXED LANGUAGES

When part of a word is from a foreign language and part is Japanese, the foreign portion is written in *KATAKANA*, and the Japanese part in *HIRAGANA* (or *KANJI*). Practice writing the following examples:

AMERIKAJIN ("American")

アメリカじん

DOITSUGO ("German lang.")

ドイツご

RŌMAJI (Roman alphabet)

ローマじ

SOREN (Soviet Union)

ソれん

KASHŪ (California)

カしゅう

KYANPU O SURU ("to camp")

キャンプをする

ABBREVIATION AND CREATIVITY

Often a foreign word transliterated into Japanese will become very long and unwieldy, and so it will be abbreviated to make it more comfortable to say. Note the following popular examples:

WĀPRO ("word processor")

ワープロ

WAISHATSU ("white shirt")

ワイシャツ

INFURE ("inflation")

インフレ

SANDO ("sandwich")

サンド

DEPĀTO ("dept. store")

デパート

ROSU ("Los Angeles")

ロス

Also, because there are many foreign language sounds and sound combinations that do not exist in Japanese, *KATAKANA* must sometimes be used very creatively to approximate the foreign sound most accurately. Practice writing the words below, paying special attention to how the foreign sound combinations are represented.

ŪRU ("wool")

ウール

UŌTĀ ("water")

ウォーター

DIZUNIIRANDO ("Disneyland")

ディズニーランド

FuASSHON ("fashion")

ファッション

FuŌKU ("fork")

フォーク

FuIRUMU ("film")

フィルム

(NOTE: Words such as these are usually either written in *KATAKANA* or spelled the usual English way, rather than romanized character for character as above.)

Of course, when there are two or more foreign words together, especially in a person's full name or the name of a company, it may be difficult to tell where one word ends and the next begins. The Japanese will often use a solid dot (•), centered in the space between the words or names, to indicate the break. Practice the following names in the spaces provided.

HOTTO DOGGU ("hot dog")   *MIKKI MAUSU* ("M. Mouse")   *JON SUMISU* ("John Smith")

ホット・ドッグ	ミッキー・マウス	ジョン・スミス

FORŌ ZA RĪDĀ ("Follow the Leader")   *NASHONAL SĀBISU* ("National Service [Co.]")

フォロー・ザ・リーダー	ナショナル・サービス

Note that when a foreign name is written with the person's middle initial, the initial is written in *RŌMAJI* and usually separated from the other two names by a solid dot, as in:

JON G. SUMISU ("John G. Smith")

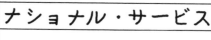

ジョン・G・スミス

Foreign names often require creativity to write them in *KATAKANA*. Try to guess what common Western names are written in *KATAKANA* below. (Correct answers are given at the bottom of the page.)

1. デービッド	2. レイモンド	3. キャロリン
4. シャーリー	5. スミス	6. ジョンソン
7. アンダーソン	8. トンプソン	9. ロバーツ
10. ホワイト	11. カーター	12. ランプキン

Keep in mind that relatively few foreign words used by the Japanese have been standardized as to how they may be written in *KATAKANA,* and you may find some of the examples presented here written slightly differently. Names, in particular, may be represented in various ways.

CORRECT ANSWERS TO NAME QUIZ: 1. David 2. Raymond 3. Caroline 4. Sherry 5. Smith 6. Johnson 7. Anderson 8. Thompson 9. Roberts 10. White 11. Carter 12. Lampkin

WRITING SENTENCES

Although *KATAKANA* is used primarily for words of foreign origin, it is possible to use it for anything Japanese as well. The rules for writing sentences are exactly the same for *KATAKANA* as for *HIRAGANA,* including the particles, spaces, punctuation, underlining, etc., with one exception; that is, the repetition symbols taught on page 35 are not used for words of foreign origin.

Review the information given on pages 32 - 35, then return to this page and proceed with the exercises that follow in the Practice and Self-Test section.

PRACTICE & SELF-TEST

On the following pages are exercises to help you practice reading and writing in *KATAKANA.*

Follow the instructions carefully. Some of the exercises require that you TRACE, COPY, and then ROMANIZE sentences given for you in *KATAKANA.* Other exercises require that you write in *KATAKANA* sentences that are presented in *ROMAJI.*

In some exercises, the *KATAKANA* is presented in machine-made characters; in others it is handwritten. Some exercises are written horizontally, some are written vertically. Every effort has been made to give you experience in a variety of writing situations, as well as to expose you to some slightly different handwriting styles.

After you have finished each exercise, check your work carefully against the correct responses given in Appendix C in the back of this book. Translations of the sentences used in this section are given in Appendix D.

If you have questions regarding the material in this workbook, feel free to ask your instructor. If you are not currently involved in a class and no instructor is available, you may call or write Lamplight's Japanese Instruction Office. The address and phone number are on page 4.

First, TRACE the following sentences, then COPY them, character for character, in the first blank space for each line. In the second blank space, ROMANIZE what you have written.

リ タ ナ カ サ ン ハ ド ノ ヨ ウ ナ

ヒ ト デ ス カ 。 ³⁾ ワ タ ク シ ハ

チ イ サ イ ア パ ー ト ニ ス ン デ

イ マ ス 。 ³⁾ シャ チョ ウ サ ン ハ ス テ キ

ナ ヒ ト デ ス ネ 。 ⁴⁾ サ ク バ ン

ノ カ イ ハ オ ソ カ ッ タ デ ス

カ 。 ⁵⁾ コ ノ ダ イ ガ ク ニ ハ ド ノ

ヨ ウ ナ ヒ ト ガ イ マ ス カ 。

Check your work against correct responses given in Appendix C.

First, TRACE the following sentences, then COPY them, character for character, in the first blank space for each line. In the second blank space, ROMANIZE what you have written.

リタ ナカサン ハ ケサ ナンジ ニ

キ マ シ タ カ。 ²⁾ワ タ ク シ ハ シャ

チョ ウ サ ン ガ ハ ワ イ ニ イ ク

ト オ モ イ マ ス。 ³⁾カ レ ガ ハ チ

ジ マ デ マッ ト オ モ イ マ セ ン。

⁴⁾モ ウ デ ン ワ ヲ シ タ ト オ

モ イ マ ス。 ⁵⁾オ カ ア サ ン ハ マ ダ゛

カ イ モ ノ ヲ シ マ セ ン デ シ タ。

Check your work against correct responses given in Appendix C.

First, TRACE the following sentences, then COPY them, character for character, in the first blank space for each line. In the second blank space, ROMANIZE what you have written.

リ ワタクシ ハ ハンカガイ ニ イ

ッテ カイモノ ヲ シマシタ。 ²⁾ハ

ワイ ニ イク トキ トモダチ ノ

ウチ ニ トマリマス。 ³⁾エイガ ヲ

ミル コト ガ スキ デス。 ⁴⁾オ

カアサン ハ ソコ ニ イッテ カ

エリマシタ。 ⁵⁾キャンプ ヲ スル コ

ト ハ タノシイ ト オモイマス。

Check your work against correct responses given in Appendix C.

First, TRACE the following sentences, then COPY them, character for character, in the first blank space for each line. In the second blank space, ROMANIZE what you have written.

リ ム コ ウ 　 ニ 　 ス ワ ッ テ 　 イ ル 　 ヒ ト

ハ 　 ダ レ 　 デ ス 　 カ 。 ³⁾ コ ン バ ン

エ イ ガ 　 ニ 　 イ キ タ イ 　 ト 　 オ モ イ

マ ス 。 ³⁾ ワ タ ク シ 　 ハ 　 ト モ ダ チ

ト 　 ベ ン キ ョ ウ 　 シ タ イ 　 ト 　 オ モ イ

マ ス 。 ⁴⁾ キ ョ ウ シ ツ 　 デ 　 ハ ナ シ タ

ヒ ト 　 ハ 　 ダ レ 　 デ シ タ 　 カ 。 ⁵⁾ キ

ノ ウ 　 ナ ニ モ 　 シ タ ク ナ カ ッ タ 　 デ ス 。

Check your work against correct responses given in Appendix C.

First, TRACE the following sentences, then COPY them, character for character, in the first blank space for each line. In the second blank space, ROMANIZE what you have written.

リ チョット ハ ナ シ テ モ イ イ デ ス

カ。 ²ⁱ アシタ マデ デンワ シ

ナクテ モ イイ デス カ。 ³ⁱ 木

ンヤ デ タベテ ハ イ ケ マ セン。

⁴ⁱ シャ チョウサン ト ハ ナサナクテ

ハ イケマセン。 ⁵ⁱ マイニチ クス

リ ヲ ノ マナクテ ハ ダメ デ

ス。 ⁶ⁱ モウ カエッテ モ イイ デス。

First, TRACE the following sentences, then COPY them, character for character, in the blank space to the right of each line. Then ROMANIZE them on the blank horizontal lines at the bottom.

1.

trace	copy	trace	copy	trace	copy	trace	copy	trace	copy	trace	copy	trace	copy	trace	copy

コドモ ハ ヒジョウ ニ カシコイ デス。

10. シゴト ハ タクサン アリマシタ カラ、オソクナリマシタ。 11. アノ

9. オトウサン ハ カレ ガ スキ デス ノデ、カネモチ ニ シマシタ。

リ ヤスクナイ デス。 8. カノジョ ハ ケサ ビョウキ ニ ナリマシタ。

ウ イウ アパート ニ スンデ イマス カ。 7. ベンリ デス ガ アマ

クナイ デス、ネ。 5. タナカサン ハ ゲンキ ナ ヒト デス。 6. ド

ジョ ノ オネエサン ハ ウツクシイ デス ケレドモ、アマリ ヤサシ

ムズカシカッタ デス。 3. キョウ ハ スゴク サムイ デス。 4. カノ

アナタ ノ クルマ ハ オオキイ デス カ。 2. キノウ ノ テスト ハ

Romanize:
_____
_____
_____
_____
_____
_____
_____

Check your work against the correct responses in Appendix C.

First, TRACE the following sentences, then COPY them, character for character, in the blank space to the right of each line. Then ROMANIZE them on the blank horizontal lines at the bottom.

trace | copy | trace | copy | trace | copy | trace | copy | trace | copy | trace | copy | trace | copy | trace | copy | trace | copy

1.
オレンジイロ ノ ハナ モ キイロ ノ ハナ モ アリマス。 2. ナラウ

ヨリ、 ナレ ヲ。 3. カノジョ ハ リンゴ ガ スキ ダ ト イイマ

シタ。 4. オカネ ガ ナイ カラ、 カイモノ ガ デキマセン。 5. コレ

ハ トショカン デハナイ ト オモイマス。 6. カノジョ ハ ニホン

ニ イッタ ト イイマシタ。 7. トウキョウ ノ デパート ヘ イキマシ

タ ガ、 ナニモ カイマセン デシタ。 8. カレラ ガ トモダチ ト タ

ベテ イナカッタ ト イイマシタ。 9. カレ ノ ニホンゴ ハ アマリ

ジョウズ デハナイ ト オモイマス。 10. キョウ アナタ ハ ナニ ヲ

シマシタ カ。 11. ケサ ゴハン ヲ タベテ、 ガッコウ ヘ イキマシタ。

Romanize:

_____

_____

_____

_____

_____

_____

Check your work against the correct responses in Appendix C.

First, TRACE the following sentences, then COPY them, character for character, in the blank space to the right of each line. Then ROMANIZE them on the blank horizontal lines at the bottom.

1.

trace	copy	trace	copy	trace	copy	trace	copy	trace	copy	trace	copy	trace	copy	trace	copy

1. ニホンショク ヲ タベタクナカッタ カラ、 トモダチ ト ショクドウ ヘ イキマセン デシタ。

2. アナタ ハ ナンジ ニ タベタイ ト オモ イマス カ。

3. ヨジ マデ ニ デンワ ヲ シナクテ ハ イケナイ ト オモイマス。

4. モウ デンワ ヲ シテ モ イイ デス カ。

5. ヨク ガンバラナクテ ハ ダメ デス ヨ。

6. ココ デ タバコ ヲ ノンデ モ イイ ト オモイマス カ。

7. ナニモ シナクテ モ イイ デス カ。

8. オトモダチ ガ ウンテン シテ ハ ダメ デス。

9. オトウサン ガ コナクテ ハ イケマセン。

10. キョウ モ アシタ モ ベンキョウ シ ナクテ ハ イケマセン。

Romanize:

_____

_____

_____

_____

_____

_____

Check your work against the correct responses in Appendix C.

First, TRACE the following sentences, then COPY them, character for character, in the blank space to the right of each line. Then ROMANIZE them on the blank horizontal lines at the bottom.

trace	copy	trace	copy	trace	copy	trace	copy	trace	copy	trace	copy	trace	copy	trace	copy	trace	copy

1.

フユ ニ ナッテ、スキー ヲ シマシタ。
2. アノ ヒト ハ ニホンジン デ エイゴ ガ デキマセン。
3. カレラ ハ イッショウケンメイ ニ ハタライテ イマス。
4. シャチョウサン ハ ヒジョウ ニ タイセツ ナ ヨウジ ガ アル ト イイマシタ。
5. カノジョ ハ ホントウ ニ キレイ デス。
6. コンバン ワタクシ ハ エイガ ニ イキタイ ト オモイマス ガ イッショ ニ イッテ クダサイマセン カ。
7. タノシミ ニ シテ イマス。
8. ユウビンキョク デ ハタライテ イル キレイ ナ オンナ ノ ヒト ハ ダレ デス カ。
9. ワタクシ ハ キョウ ナニ モ シタクナイ ト オモイマス。

Romanize:

_____

_____

_____

_____

_____

_____

_____

First, COPY each line below onto the first blank space beneath it. In the second blank space write the line in *RŌMAJI*. Check your work carefully with Appendix C.

1. アイス・クリーム を たべましょう か。   2. きのう の

copy _____

rōmaji _____

テスト は むずかしかった です、ネ！   3. この アパー

copy _____

rōmaji _____

ト は あまり べんり では ありません。   4. アパート

copy _____

rōmaji _____

を きれい に して ください。   5. オレンジいろ の く

copy _____

rōmaji _____

るま は わたくし の です。   6. アメリカじん は いつ

copy _____

rōmaji _____

も サンドイッチ を たべる と いいました。   7. かれ

copy _____

rōmaji _____

は サン・フランシスコ へ いきました けれども、 ロス

copy _____

rōmaji _____

へ いきません でした。   8. テレビ を みて いた とき、

copy _____

rōmaji _____

ポップコーン を たべました。

copy _____

rōmaji _____

First, COPY each line below onto the first blank space beneath it. In the second blank space write the line in *ROMAJI.* Check your work carefully with Appendix C.

1. おにいさん は ニュー・ヨーク に すんで います が、

copy _____

romaji _____

フランス で べんきょう しました。 2. やま まで ヒッ

copy _____

romaji _____

チハイク を して、 キャンプ を しました。 3. ハワイ

copy _____

romaji _____

へ いく とき、 ホノルル の ホテル に とまります。

copy _____

romaji _____

4. ホワイトさん は スペインじん の おともだち が ら

copy _____

romaji _____

いしゅう くる と いいました。 5. いま L・A・タイム

copy _____

romaji _____

ズ を よんで いる ひと は スミスさん です。 6. しろ

copy _____

romaji _____

い セーター を きて いる ハワイじん は 「スター・ウ

copy _____

romaji _____

オーズ」 と いう えいが を みて きました。

copy _____

romaji _____

Write the following sentences completely in *KATAKANA.* Check your work carefully against the correct responses given in Appendix C.

1. *TANAKA-SAN WA GENKI NA HITO DESU, NE.*

2. *DŌ IU APĀTO NI SUNDE IMASU KA.*

3. *BENRI DESU GA, AMARI ŌKIKUNAI DESU.*

4. *KYŌ WA HAYAKU ATSUKUNARIMASHITA.*

5. *MUKŌ NO OTOKO NO HITO WA ISSHŌKENMEI NI HATARAITE IMASU.*

6. *KAI WA ZENZEN OMOSHIROKUNAKATTA DESU YO.*

7. *ANATA WA NIHONSHOKU GA SUKI DESU KA?*

8. *ICHIBAN SUKI NA IRO WA NANIIRO DESU KA?*

9. *ONIISAN WA KINŌ UCHI NI KAETTA TOKI, NANI O SHIMASHITA KA?*

10. *BUCHŌ-SAN GA ATARASHII KURUMA O KATTA TO IIMASHITA.*

11. *KANOJO WA UTAU KOTO GA DEKIRU TO OMOIMASEN.*

12. *KARE NO KURUMA GA AKAI TO ITTA TO OMOIMASU.*

Write the following sentences completely in *KATAKANA*. Check your work carefully against the correct responses given in Appendix C.

1.   *KARE WA KYŌ SHIGOTO NI IKANAKATTA DESU.*

   ┌───┐
   │   │
   └───┘

2.   *ANO HITO WA JIMUSHO NI KONAKATTA TO OMOIMASU.*

   ┌───┐
   │   │
   └───┘

3.   *SAKUBAN NO KAI WA NAGAKUNAKUTE YOKATTA DESU.*

   ┌───┐
   │   │
   └───┘

4.   *ANO HON WA BETSU NI OMOSHIROKUNAI DESU.*

   ┌───┐
   │   │
   └───┘

5.   *DOYŌBI WATAKUSHI WA OJIISAN NO TOKORO E IKIMASHITA.*

   ┌───┐
   │   │
   └───┘

6.   *KANOJO WA MAINICHI DAIGAKU DE HATARAKIMASU.*

   ┌───┐
   │   │
   └───┘

7.   *ANATA WA NANI GA HOSHII TO OMOIMASU KA?*

   ┌───┐
   │   │
   └───┘

8.   *ENPITSU GA HITSUYŌ DA TO IIMASHITA.*

   ┌───┐
   │   │
   └───┘

9.   *ANO HITO WA EKI O SAGASHITE IRU TO IIMASHITA.*

   ┌───┐
   │   │
   └───┘

10. *HON'YA E ITTE, OKĀSAN NO TANONDA HON O KAIMASHITA.*

   ┌───┐
   │   │
   └───┘

11. *MŌ KAETTE MO II DESU KA?*

   ┌───┐
   │   │
   └───┘

12. *GETSUYŌBI NI MATA GAKKŌ E IKANAKEREBA NARIMASEN.*

   ┌───┐
   │   │
   └───┘

Write the following sentences in *KANA,* using *KATAKANA* for words of foreign origin and *HIRAGANA* for everything else. Check your work carefully against the correct responses given in Appendix C.

1. *SUMISU SENSEI NO ONĒSAN WA HAWAI NI SUNDE IMASU.*

2. *WATAKUSHI NO KAMERA WA DAME NI NARIMASHITA.*

3. *MAZUI HANBĀGĀ O TABEMASHITA NODE, BYŌKI NI NARIMASHITA.*

4. *ORENJIIRO NO SĒTĀ O KITE IRU HITO WA O-TOMODACHI DESU KA?*

5. *KARE WA AMERIKA NO GINKŌ DE HATARAITE IMASU.*

6. *ASHITA DEPĀTO E ITTE, MIKKI MAUSU NO TOKEI O KAIMASU.*

7. *TOMODACHI WA FURANSU NO DAIGAKU DE BENKYŌ SHITE IMASU.*

8. *RANCHI GA OWATTE, SŪPĀ NI IKITAI TO OMOIMASU.*

9. *OKĀSAN WA BASU DE HANKAGAI E IKIMASHITA.*

10. *SUTĒKI TO SARADA O CHŪMON SHIMASHITA KA?*

11. *KOKO DE TABAKO O NONDE MO II DESU KA?*

12. *EIGAKAN NI ITTE, "SHINDERERA" TO IU EIGA O MIMASHITA.*

Write the following sentences in *KANA,* using *KATAKANA* for words of foreign origin and *HIRAGANA* for everything else. Check your work carefully against the correct responses given in Appendix C.

1. *ANO PEN WA JŪ-DORU YONJŪGO-SENTO DE TAKAI DESU.*

2. *KARE WA SUĒDENJIN DE, FURANSUGO TO DOITSUGO O HANASHIMASU.*

3. *IMA SUKII O SHITE INAI HITO WA BYŌKI DESU KA?*

4. *AISU KURIIMU GA DAISUKI DE, MAINICHI TABEMASU.*

5. *SUNAKKU E ITTE, SANDOITCHI O TABEMASHŌ KA?*

6. *TAKUSHII DE ITTE KIMASHITA KA?*

7. *SĒRU GA ATTA KARA, OKĀSAN WA SŪPĀ NI IKIMASHITA.*

8. *GASORIN GA NAI KARA, KURUMA O UNTEN DEKIMASEN.*

9. *NANPEIJI MADE YOMIMASHITA KA?*

10. *RAJIO O KIITE IRU HITO WA MEKISHIKOJIN DA TO OMOIMASU.*

11. *SUMISU-SAN TO BURAUN-SAN WA YŌROPPA DE RYOKŌ O SHITE IMASU.*

12. *HOTERU NO RESUTORAN DE SHOKUJI O SHIMASHITA.*

A P P E N D I X   A: MACHINE-MADE CHARACTERS *(cf. pp. 4-27 and 53-72)*

HIRAGANA

GOJŪON

わ	ら	や	ま	は	な	た	さ	か	あ
	り		み	ひ	に	ち	し	き	い
	る	ゆ	む	ふ	ぬ	つ	す	く	う
	れ		め	へ	ね	て	せ	け	え
を	ろ	よ	も	ほ	の	と	そ	こ	お
ん									

VOICED & BILABIALIZED

が	ぎ	ぐ	げ	ご
ざ	じ	ず	ぜ	ぞ
だ	ぢ	づ	で	ど
ば	び	ぶ	べ	ぼ
ぱ	ぴ	ぷ	ぺ	ぽ

COMBINATION CHARACTERS

りゃ	みゃ	ぴゃ	びゃ	ひゃ	にゃ	ぢゃ	ちゃ	じゃ	しゃ	ぎゃ	きゃ
りゅ	みゅ	ぴゅ	びゅ	ひゅ	にゅ	ぢゅ	ちゅ	じゅ	しゅ	ぎゅ	きゅ
りょ	みょ	ぴょ	びょ	ひょ	にょ	ぢょ	ちょ	じょ	しょ	ぎょ	きょ

KATAKANA

GOJŪON

ワ	ラ	ヤ	マ	ハ	ナ	タ	サ	カ	ア
	リ		ミ	ヒ	ニ	チ	シ	キ	イ
	ル	ユ	ム	フ	ヌ	ツ	ス	ク	ウ
	レ		メ	ヘ	ネ	テ	セ	ケ	エ
ヲ	ロ	ヨ	モ	ホ	ノ	ト	ソ	コ	オ
ン									

VOICED & BILABIALIZED

ガ	ギ	グ	ゲ	ゴ
ザ	ジ	ズ	ゼ	ソ
ダ	ヂ	ヅ	デ	ド
バ	ビ	ブ	ベ	ボ
パ	ピ	プ	ペ	ポ

COMBINATION CHARACTERS

リャ	ミャ	ピャ	ビャ	ヒャ	ニャ	ヂャ	チャ	ジャ	シャ	ギャ	キャ
リュ	ミュ	ピュ	ビュ	ヒュ	ニュ	ヂュ	チュ	ジュ	シュ	ギュ	キュ
リョ	ミョ	ピョ	ビョ	ヒョ	ニョ	ヂョ	チョ	ジョ	ショ	ギョ	キョ

APPENDIX B: EXCEPTIONS IN *KANA*

1.   EXCEPTIONAL LONG "O"   *(cf. p. 30)*

In some words the vowel sound /O/ is elongated by the character お *(O)* rather than う *(U)*.

For your information, these exceptional words were anciently written with *HO* (ほ) as the second *O;* for example, おおい *(ŌI)* was once written おほい *(OHOI)*. Since it is impossible to tell from the word itself whether it falls into this category or not, it is necessary to memorize the exceptions. There are only a few, the most common of which are listed here.

HŌ ほお	*KŌRI* こおり	*TŌ* とお	*ŌU* おおう
"cheek"	"ice"	"ten"	"to cover"

TŌI とおい	*TŌRI / DŌRI* とおり どおり	*TŌRU* とおる
"far away"	"street," "road," "highway"	"to pass through"

Also, any time the word begins with the prefix *Ō,* meaning "big," this exception applies:

ŌKII おおきい	*ŌSAKA* おおさか	*ŌKAMI* おおかみ	*ŌHASHI* おおはし
"big"	the city "Osaka"	"wolf"	"big bridge"

2.   EXCEPTIONAL *JI* AND *ZU*   *(cf. p. 15, notes 2 & 3)*

The voiced characters ぢ *(JI)* and づ *(ZU)* are used only occasionally and in the following instances:

A.   when the word originally used the character ち or つ but became voiced when combined with another word to make a compound, such as —

KOZUTSUMI こづつみ   *(TSUTSUMI* = "package" ; *KO* = "small")
"postal package"

HANAJI はなぢ   *(CHI* = "blood" ; *HANA* = "nose")
"nosebleed"

B.   when the voiced character is a repetition of its unvoiced counterpart, as in —

CHIJIMU ちぢむ
"to shrink"

TSUZUKU つづく
"to continue"

Note: The word *ICHINICHIJŪ,* which is a compound of *ICHINICHI* ("one day") and *CHŪ* ("center") and means "all day long," is written in this book with ぢゅ, according to rule A above. However, current common usage leans toward writing this word with じゅ: いちにちじゅう

A P P E N D I X   C: CORRECT RESPONSES TO PRACTICE & SELF-TEST EXERCISES

PAGE 37

1. KORE WA NAN DESU KA? 2. SORE WA TOKEI DESU. 3. ANO HITO WA DARE DESU KA? 4. KANOJO WA TANAKA-SAN DESU. 5. SHOKUDO WA ASOKO DESU KA? 6. O-TEARAI WA DOKO DESU KA? 7. KARE WA SENSEI DEWA ARIMASEN. 8. ANO HITO WA GAIJIN DESU KA? 9. YUBINKYOKU WA MUKO DESU. 10. WATAKUSHI WA GAKUSEI DESHITA. 11. IRIGUCHI WA ASOKO DESU, NE?

PAGE 38

1. NAN DESU KA? 2. TOSHOKAN WA DOKO NI ARIMASU KA? 3. GINKO WA MUKO NI ARIMASU. 4. JUGYOIN WA DOKO NI IMASU KA? 5. JUGYOIN WA ANO HEYA NI IMASU. 6. ANO HEYA NI WA GOMIBAKO GA ARIMASU KA? 7. KYOSHITSU NI TSUKUE GA ARIMASEN. 8. ANO HEYA NI DARE GA IMASHITA KA? 9. KARE WA IMASEN.

PAGE 39

1. YOKU IRASSHAIMASHITA. 2. DOKO E IKIMASU KA? 3. KESA GAKKO NI KIMASHITA. 4. KINO TANAKA-SAN WA JIMUSHO NI KIMASEN DESHITA. 5. SHACHO-SAN WA KYO TAKUSHII DE KAERIMASHITA. 6. ANATA WA MO KAERIMASU KA? 7. KANOJO WA NAN DE TOKYO NI IKIMASHITA KA? 8. WATAKUSHI WA KINO YUBINKYOKU E IKIMASEN DESHITA. 9. KARE WA TOMODACHI DESU.

PAGE 40

1. ANO HITO WA NIHONGO O BENKYO SHITE IMASU KA? 2. SHACHO-SAN NI MO ICHIDO DENWA O SHITE KUDASAI. 3. KANOJO WA SHINBUN O YONDE IMASEN. 4. TANAKA-SAN WA KURUMA O YUBINKYOKU MADE UNTEN SHIMASHITA. 5. WATAKUSHI WA HON'YA E IKIMASHITA KEREDOMO, HON O KAIMASEN DESHITA. 6. KYO WATAKUSHI TO TABETE KUDASAIMASEN KA?

PAGE 41

1. ANATA WA NAZE KYOSHITSU NI IKIMASEN KA? 2. ASHITA MADE DENWA SHINAIDE KUDASAI. 3. RAISHU MATA KURU KOTO GA DEKIMASU KA? 4. KONBAN ISOGASHII DESU KARA, IKU KOTO GA DEKIMASEN. 5. O-KYAKU-SAMA GA SUGU KIMASU NODE, MADA KAERANAIDE KUDASAI. 6. ONIISAN WA NAZE TABEMASEN DESHITA KA? 7. JUICHIJI MADE BENKYO SHIMASHO, NE?

PAGE 42

1. DO IU IMI DESU KA? 2. SHITSUMON GA ARIMASU KA? 3. OHAYO GOZAIMASU. 4. OYASUMI NASAI. 5. AA, SO DESU KA? 6. DEWA MATA. 7. WAKARIMASU, DESHO? 8. SAYONARA. 9. IKURA DESU KA? 10. ICHIMANGOSEN-NIHYAKUJU-DORU DESU. 11. TAKAI DESU, NE? 12. IIE, YASUI DESU YO. 13. O-NAMAE WA NAN DESU KA? 14. TANAKA TO MOSHIMASU. 15. HAJIMEMASHITE. 16. YOROSHIKU O-NEGAI SHIMASU. 17. DOMO ARIGATO GOZAIMASU. 18. DO ITASHIMASHITE. 19. KYUHYAKUROKUJUGOEN DESU.

PAGE 43

1. DEGUCHI WA DOKO DESU KA? 2. IRIGUCHI WA MUKO DESU, NE? 3. KARE WA SENSEI DEWA ARIMASEN KA? 4. WATAKUSHI NO DAIGAKU WA TOKYO NI ARIMASU. 5. ANATA NO TSUKUE WA DORE DESU KA? 6. ZANNEN DESU, NE? 7. JIMUSHO NI WA GOMIBAKO MO TOKEI MO ARIMASU. 8. DONO HEYA GA KARE NO DESU KA? 9. KYOSHITSU NI WA, SENSEI MO GAKUSEI MO IMASU. 10. SHACHO-SAN TO JUGYOIN WA IMA SONO HEYA NI IMASU KA? 11. ANATA NO KURUMA WA MUKO NI ARIMASEN DESHITA.

PAGE 44

1. IRASSHAIMASE. 2. KONDO WA ISSHO NI IKIMASHO. 3. SENSHU YUBINKYOKU E IKIMASHITA KA? 4. RAISHU MAINICHI ONESAN TO ISSHO NI CHIKATETSU DE KAERIMASU. 5. GO-CHISO-SAMA DESHITA. 6. CHOTTO MATTE KUDASAI. 7. ITTE KIMASU. 8. OKASAN TO ONESAN TO ISSHO NI SHOKUDO DE TABETE IMASHITA. 9. KARE WA JUJI JUGOFUN MAE NI KAERIMASHITA. 10. SAKUBAN DAIGAKU NO DEGUCHI DE TANAKA-SAN TO MATTE IMASHITA. 11. OTOTO WA OSAKA DE HATARAITE IMASU KA? 12. IMOTO WA IMA HEYA DE TEGAMI O YONDE IMASU.

PAGE 45

1. O-JAMA SHIMASU. 2. O-TANJOBI O-MEDETO GOZAIMASU. 3. ITSUMO DOKO DE KYUKEI O SHIMASU KA? 4. ICHINICHIJU BENKYO SURU KOTO GA DEKIMASEN DESHITA. 5. OKANE GA ARIMASEN NODE, MADA HON O KAWANAIDE KUDASAI. 6. MINNA WA NIHONGO GA DEKIMASU KA? 7. OTOSAN WA KOTOSHI NIHON DE RYOKO O SHITE IMASU. 8. ASHITA NO ASA, GAKKO DE SENSEI TO HANASHITE KUDASAIMASEN KA? 9. O-NAKA GA SUITE IMASU KEREDOMO, MADA SHOKUJI GA DEKIMASEN. 10. GETSUYOBI WA KYUJITSU DESU KARA, WATAKUSHI-TACHI WA SHIGOTO E IKIMASEN.

PAGE 46

TANAKA: "SENSEI WA KYOSHITSU NI IMASU KA?"
HONDA: "IIE, JIMUSHO NI IMASU."
TANAKA: "JIMUSHO WA DOKO NI ARIMASU KA?"
HONDA: "MUKO NI ARIMASU."
TANAKA: "KONO HEN NI WA GOMIBAKO GA ARIMASU KA?"
HONDA: "GOMIBAKO WA ANO HEYA NI ARIMASU."
TANAKA: "O-TEARAI MO ARIMASU KA?"
HONDA: "IIE, ARIMASEN. TOSHOKAN NI ARIMASU."
TANAKA: "DOMO ARIGATO GOZAIMASU."

PAGE 47

SATO: "O-TOMODACHI NI DENWA O SHIMASHO KA?"
AKI: "KYO IMASEN KARA, MADA SHINAIDE KUDASAI."
SATO: "HAI, WAKARIMASHITA. DEWA, TOSHOKAN E IKIMASHO KA?"
AKI: "SUMIMASEN GA, KYO ISOIDE IMASU NODE, DEKIMASEN. GOMEN NASAI, NE?"
SATO: "II DESU YO. ASHITA WA DO DESU KA?"
AKI: "HAI, ASHITA WA KEKKO DESU YO."

PAGE 48

1. それ は あなた の ほん です か。 2. かれ は せんせい では ありません でした。 3. としょかん は むこう です。 4. あなた は がくせい では ありません か。 5. ゆうびんきょく は どれ です か。 6. それ は かのじょ の じしょ です、ね。 7. あの ひと の つくえ は あそこ です。 8. たなかさん の とけい は たかい、でしょう。 9. あの ひとびと は だいがくせい でした。 10. むこう の ひと は しゃちょうさん です、ね。 11. ほんやさん は がいじん です。 12. わたくしたち は にほんじん では ありません。

PAGE 49

1. おともだち は いま しょくどう に います。 2. おてあらい は どこ に あります か。 3. わたくし は くるま が ありません。 4. かのじょ は せんしゅう とうきょう に いました。 5. せいとたち は きのう きょうしつ に いま

(Continued on next page.)

(Page 49, continued.)

せん でした。 6．あの へや に は だれ が います か。 7．この じてんしゃ は かれ の では ありません。 8．じゅうぎょういん も しゃちょうさん も じむしょ に います。 9．ごみばこ も おてあらい に あります か。 10．あの ひとびと は きのう の あさ ゆうびんきょく に いました。 11．しょくどう は あそこ に あります、ね。 12．ぎんこう も としょかん も そこ に あります。

PAGE 50

1．あなた は きょう としょかん に いきます か。 2．ゆうべ しょくどう へ いきません でした。 3．しゃちょうさん は ひこうき で とうきょう へ いきました、でしょう。 4．おねえさん は まいにち ちかてつ で かえります。 5．せんげつ みんな は でんしゃ で きました。 6．らいねん ふね で いきましょう。 7．おにいさん と いっしょに きました、ね。 8．いま わたくし は じかん が ありません。 9．いもうとさん は もう かえりました か。 10．おともだち は ひこうき で ちゅうごく へ かえりました か。 11．ごしゅじん は さくばん の かい に いきました か。 12．たなかさん は あした さっぽろ へ かえります。

PAGE 51

1．あなた は いま なに を して います か。 2．かれ の りょうしん は おおさか に すんで います。 3．かのじょ は へや で てがみ を かいて います。 4．おにいさん と おとうさん は いっしょに はしって いました。 5．おともだち と むこう に すわって ください。 6．みんな は もう うち へ かえって います。 7．すこし べんきょう して くださいません か。 8．としょかん へ いきます けれども、べんきょう しません。 9．たなかさん は けさ むこう に たって いました。 10．かのじょたち は まだ きゅうけい を して います。 11．あの うた を うたって くださいます か。 12．わたくし は ぎんこう で はたらいて いません でした。

PAGE 52

1．あした は きゅうじつ です から、やすんで ください。 2．にほんご を はなす こと が できます か。 3．びょうき です ので、じむしょ へ いかないで ください。 4．らいげつ の かい に いく こと が できません か。 5．かのじょ は うたう こと が できません。 6．もう すこし まつ こと が できます か。 7．たかい です ので、かわないで ください。 8．あなた は なぜ はんかがい へ いきません でした か。 9．じかん が ありません から、まだ たべないで ください。 10．きょうしつ で ともだち と はなさないで ください。 11．くるま が ありません から、でんしゃ で いきます。 12．えいご が できません ので、にほんご で はなして いました。

PAGE 78

1. TANAKA-SAN WA DONO YŌ NA HITO DESU KA?
2. WATAKUSHI WA CHIISAI APĀTO NI SUNDE IMASU.
3. SHACHŌ-SAN WA SUTEKI NA HITO DESU, NE?
4. SAKUBAN NO KAI WA OSOKATTA DESU KA?
5. KONO DAIGAKU NI WA DONO YŌ NA HITO GA IMASU KA?

PAGE 79

1. TANAKA-SAN WA KESA NANJI NI KIMASHITA KA?
2. WATAKUSHI WA SHACHŌ-SAN GA HAWAI NI IKU TO OMOIMASU. 3. KARE GA HACHIJI MADE MATSU TO OMOIMASEN. 4. MŌ DENWA O SHITA TO OMOIMASU. 5. OKASAN WA MADA KAIMONO O SHIMASEN DESHITA.

PAGE 80

1. WATAKUSHI WA HANKAGAI NI ITTE, KAIMONO O SHIMASHITA. 2. HAWAI NI IKU TOKI, TOMODACHI NO UCHI NI TOMARIMASU. 3. EIGA O MIRU KOTO GA SUKI DESU. 4. OKASAN WA SOKO NI ITTE KAERI-MASHITA. 5. KYANPU O SURU KOTO WA TANOSHII TO OMOIMASU.

PAGE 81

1. MUKŌ NI SUWATTE IRU HITO WA DARE DESU KA?
2. KONBAN EIGA NI IKITAI TO OMOIMASU. 3. WATA-KUSHI WA TOMODACHI TO BENKYO SHITAI TO OMOI-MASU. 4. KYŌSHITSU DE HANASHITA HITO WA DARE DESHITA KA? 5. KINO NANIMO SHITAKUNA-KATTA DESU.

PAGE 82

1. CHOTTO HANASHITE MO II DESU KA? 2. ASHITA MADE DENWA SHINAKUTE MO II DESU KA? 3. HON'-YA DE TABETE WA IKEMASEN. 4. SHACHŌ-SAN TO HANASANAKUTE WA IKEMASEN. 5. MAINICHI KUSU-RI O NOMANAKUTE WA DAME DESU. 6. MŌ KAETTE MO II DESU.

PAGE 83

1. ANATA NO KURUMA WA ŌKII DESU KA? 2. KINŌ NO TESUTO WA MUZUKASHIKATTA DESU. 3. KYŌ WA SUGOKU SAMUI DESU. 4. KANOJO NO ONESAN WA UTSUKUSHII DESU KEREDOMO, AMARI YASASHI-KUNAI DESU, NE? 5. TANAKA-SAN WA GENKI NA HITO DESU. 6. DŌ IU APĀTO NI SUNDE IMASU KA?
7. BENRI DESU GA, AMARI YASUKUNAI DESU.
8. KANOJO WA KESA BYŌKI NI NARIMASHITA.
9. OTOSAN WA KARE GA SUKI DESU NODE, KANE-MOCHI NI SHIMASHITA. 10. SHIGOTO WA TAKUSAN ARIMASHITA KARA, OSOKUNARIMASHITA. 11. ANO KODOMO WA HIJŌ NI KASHIKOI DESU.

PAGE 84

1. ORENJIIRO NO HANA MO KIIRO NO HANA MO ARIMASU. 2. NARAU YORI, NARE YO. 3. KANOJO WA RINGO GA SUKI DA TO IIMASHITA. 4. OKANE GA NAI KARA, KAIMONO GA DEKIMASEN. 5. KORE WA TOSHOKAN DEWANAI TO OMOIMASU. 6. KANOJO WA NIHON NI ITTA TO IIMASHITA. 7. TŌKYŌ NO DEPATO E IKIMASHITA GA, NANIMO KAIMASEN DESHI-TA. 8. KARERA GA TOMODACHI TO TABETE INA-KATTA TO IIMASHITA. 9. KARE NO NIHONGO WA AMARI JŌZU DEWANAI TO OMOIMASU. 10. KYŌ ANATA WA NANI O SHIMASHITA KA? 11. KESA GOHAN O TABETE, GAKKŌ E IKIMASHITA.

PAGE 85

1. NIHONSHOKU O TABETAKUNAKATTA KARA, TOMO-DACHI TO SHOKUDO E IKIMASEN DESHITA. 2. ANA-TA WA NANJI NI TABETAI TO OMOIMASU KA?
3. YOJI MADE NI DENWA O SHINAKUTE WA IKENAI TO OMOIMASU. 4. MŌ DENWA O SHITE MO II DESU KA? 5. YOKU GANBARANAKUTE WA DAME DESU YO.
6. KOKO DE TABAKO O NONDE MO II TO OMOIMASU KA? 7. NANIMO SHINAKUTE MO II DESU KA?
8. OTOMODACHI GA UNTEN SHITE WA DAME DESU.
9. OTOSAN GA KONAKUTE WA IKEMASEN. 10. KYŌ MO ASHITA MO BENKYŌ SHINAKUTE WA IKEMASEN.

PAGE 86

1. FUYU NI NATTE, SUKII O SHIMASHITA.
2. ANO HITO WA NIHONJIN DE EIGO GA DEKIMASEN.
3. KARERA WA ISSHŌKENMEI NI HATARAITE IMASU.
4. SHACHŌ-SAN WA HIJŌ NI TAISETSU NA YŌJI GA ARU TO IIMASHITA. 5. KANOJO WA HONTŌ NI KIREI DESU. 6. KONBAN WATAKUSHI WA EIGA NI IKITAI TO OMOIMASU GA ISSHO NI ITTE KUDASAIMASEN KA?
7. TANOSHIMI NI SHITE IMASU. 8. YŪBINKYOKU DE HATARAITE IRU KIREI NA ONNA NO HITO WA DARE DESU KA? 9. WATAKUSHI WA KYŌ NANIMO SHITA-KUNAI TO OMOIMASU.

PAGE 87

1. AISU-KURIIMU O TABEMASHŌ KA? 2. KINŌ NO TESUTO WA MUZUKASHIKATTA DESU, NE!

(Continued on next page.)

(Page 87, continued.)

3. KO<u>N</u>O APATO WA AMARI BENRI DEWA ARIMASEN.
4. AP<u>Ā</u>TO O KIREI NI SHITE KUDASAI.   5. ORENJI-IRO NO KURUMA WA WATAKUSHI NO DESU.
6. AMERIKA-JIN WA ITSUMO SANDOITCHI O TABERU TO IIMASHITA.   7. KARE WA SAN FURANSHISUKO E IKIMASHITA KEREDOMO, ROSU E IK<u>I</u>MASEN DESHITA.
8. TEREBI O MITE ITA TOKI, POPPUKO<u>N</u> O TABEMA-SHITA.

PAGE 88

1. ONIISAN WA NY<u>Ū</u> Y<u>Ō</u>KU NI SUNDE IMASU GA, FURANSU DE BENKY<u>Ō</u> SHIMASHITA.   2. YAMA MADE HITCHIHAIKU O SHITE, KYANPU O SHIMASHITA.
3. HAWAI E IKU TOKI, HONORURU NO HOTERU NI TOMARIMASU.   4. HOWAITOSAN WA SUPEINJIN NO OTOMODACHI GA RAISH<u>Ū</u> KURU TO IIMASHITA.
5. IMA L.A. TIMES (TAIMUZU) O Y<u>O</u>NDE IRU HITO WA SUMISU-SAN DESU. _ 6._SHIROI S<u>Ē</u>TĀ O KITE IRU HAWAIJIN WA "SUT<u>Ā</u> W<u>Ō</u>ZU"TO IU EIGA O MITE KIMASHITA.

PAGE 89

1．タナカサン ハ ゲンキ ナ ヒト デス、ネ。 2．ドウ イウ アパート ニ スンデ イマス カ。 3．ベンリ デス ガ、アマリ オオキクナイ デス。 4．キョウ ハ ハヤク アツクナ リマシタ。 5．ムコウ ノ オトコ ノ ヒト ハ イッショウケンメイ ニ ハタライテ イマス。 6．カイ ハ ゼンゼン オモシロクナッタ デス ヨ。 7．アナタ ハ ニホンショク ガ スキ デス カ。 8．イチバン スキ ナ イロ ハ ナニイロ デス カ。 9．オニイサン ハ キノウ ウチ ニ カエッタ トキ、ナニ ヲ シマシタ カ。 10．ブチョウサン ガ アタラシイ クルマ ヲ カッタ ト イイマシタ。 11．カノジョ ハ ウタウ コト ガ デキル ト オモイマセン。 12．カレ ノ クルマ ガ アカイ ト イッタ ト オモイマス。

PAGE 90

1．カレ ハ キョウ シゴト ニ イカナカッタ デス。 2．アノ ヒト ハ ジムショ ニ コナカッタ ト オモイマス。 3．サクバン ノ カイ ハ ナガクナクテ ヨカッタ デス。 4．アノ ホン ハ ベツ ニ オモシロクナイ デス。 5．ドヨウビ ワタクシ ハ オジイサン ノ トコロ ヘ イキマシタ。 6．カノジョ ハ マイニチ ダイガク デ ハタラキマス。 7．アナタ ハ ナニ ガ ホシイ ト オモイマス カ。 8．エンピツ ガ ヒツヨウ ダ ト イイマシタ。 9．アノ ヒト ハ エキ ヲ サガシテ イル ト イイマシタ。 10．ホンヤ ヘ イッテ、オカアサン ノ タノンダ ホン ヲ カイマシタ。 11．モウ カエッテ モ イイ デス カ。 12．ゲツヨウビ ニ マタ ガッコウ ヘ イカナケレバ ナリマセン。

PAGE 91

1．スミス せんせい の おねえさん は ハワイ に すんで います。 2．わたくし の カメラ は だめ に なりました。 3．まずい ハンバーガー を たべました ので、びょうき に なりました。 4．オレンジいろ の セーター を きて いる ひと は おともだち ですか。 5．かれ は アメリカ の ぎんこう で はたらいて います。 6．あした デパート へ いって、ミッキ・マウス の とけい を かいます。 7．ともだち は フランス の だいがく で べんきょう して います。 8．ランチ が おわって、スーパー に いきたい と おもいます。 9．おかあさん は バス で はんかがい へ いきました。 10．ステーキ と サラダ を ちゅうもん しました か。 11．ここ で タバコ を のんでも いい です か。

12．えいがかん に いって、「シンデレラ」 と いう えいが を みました。

PAGE 92

1．あの ペン は じゅうドル よんじゅうごセント で たかい です。 2．かれ は スエーデンじん で、フランスご と ドイツご を はなします。 3．いま スキー を して いない ひと は びょうき です か。 4．アイス・クリーム が だいすき で、まいにち たべます。 5．スナック へ いって、サンドイッチ を たべましょう か。 6．タクシイ で いって きました か。 7．セール が あった から、おかあさん は スーパー に いきました。 8．ガソリン が ない から、くるま を うんてん できません。 9．なんペイジ まで よみました か。 10．ラジオ を きいて いる ひと は メキシコじん だ と おもいます。 11．スミスさん と ブラウンさん は ヨーロッパ で りょこう を して います。 12．ホテル の レストラン で しょくじ を しました。

APPENDIX D: TRANSLATIONS FOR PRACTICE & SELF-TEST EXERCISES

PAGE 37

1. What is this?   2. That is a watch.   3. Who is that person?   4. She is Tanaka.   5. Is the restaurant over there?   6. Where is the lavatory?   7. He is not a teacher.   8. Is that person a foreigner?   9. The post office is over there.   10. I was a student.   11. The entrance is over there, isn't it?

PAGE 38

1. What is it?   2. Where is the library?   3. The bank is over there.   4. Where are the employees?   5. The employees are in that room.   6. Is there a wastebasket in that room?   7. There is not a desk in the classroom.   8. Who was in that room?   9. He is not [in].

PAGE 39

1. Welcome.   2. Where are you going?   3. This morning I came to school.   4. Yesterday Tanaka did not come to the office.   5. The company president returned by taxi today.   6. Are you going home already?   7. How (by means of what) did she go to Tokyo?   8. I did not go to the post office yesterday.   9. He is a friend.

PAGE 40

1. Is that person studying Japanese?   2. Please telephone the company president one more time.   3. She is not reading the newspaper.   4. Tanaka drove the car as far as the post office.   5. I went to the bookstore, but I didn't buy a book.   6. Won't you please eat with me today?

PAGE 41

1. Why don't you go to the classroom?   2. Please don't phone until tomorrow.   3. Can you come again next week?   4. I am busy tonight, so I cannot go.   5. Since guests will come soon, please don't go back yet.   6. Why did older brother not eat?   7. Let's study until 11:00.

PAGE 42

1. What does it mean?   2. Do you have a question?   3. Good morning.   4. Good night.   5. Is that right?   6. See you later.   7. You understand, don't you?   8. Goodbye.   9. How much is it?   10. It is $15,210.   11. It is expensive, isn't it?   12. No, it's cheap!   13. What is your name?   14. I am called Tanaka.   15. Please to meet you.   16. Please accept my regards.   17. Thank you very much.   18. Think nothing of it.   19. It is 960 yen.

PAGE 43

1. Where is the exit?   2. The entrance is over there, isn't it?   3. Is he not a teacher?   4. My university is in Tokyo.   5. Which one is your desk?   6. That's too bad, isn't it?   7. In the office there is both a wastebasket and a clock.   8. Which room is his?   9. In the classroom there are both teachers and students.   10. Are the company president and the employees in that room now?   11. Your car was not over there.

PAGE 44

1. Welcome. / Come in.   2. Let's go together next time.   3. Did you go to the post office last week?   4. Next week I will go home with older sister by subway every day.   5. Thank you for the meal.   6. Please wait a moment.   7. I'll be right back.   8. Mother and older sister were eating together in the restaurant.   9. He went home at fifteen minutes till ten.   10. I was waiting with Tanaka at the university exit last night.   11. Is younger brother working in Osaka?   12. Younger sister is reading a letter in [her] room now.

PAGE 45

1. Excuse me for bothering you.   2. Happy birthday.   3. Where do you always take [your] break?   4. I was not able to study all day long.   5. Please don't buy the book yet, because there is no money.   6. Can everyone [speak] Japanese?   7. Father is travelling in Japan this year.   8. Won't you please speak with the teacher at school tomorrow morning?   9. I am hungry, but I cannot have dinner yet.   10. Since Monday is a holiday, we won't go to work.

PAGE 46

TANAKA: "Is the teacher in the classroom?"
HONDA: "No, he is in the office."
TANAKA: "Where is the office?"
HONDA: "It is over there."
TANAKA: "Is there a wastebasket around here?"
HONDA: "The wastebasket is in that room."
TANAKA: "Is there a lavatory, also?"
HONDA: "No, there isn't. It is in the library."
TANAKA: "Thank you very much."

PAGE 47

SATO: "Shall we phone your friend?"
AKI: "He isn't in today, so please don't do it yet."
SATO: "Yes, I understand. (It is understood.) Well, shall we go to the library?"
AKI: "Excuse me, but I can't today, because I am busy. I'm sorry."
SATO: "That's okay! How about tomorrow?"
AKI: "Yes, tomorrow will be splendid!"

PAGE 48

1. Is that your book?   2. He was not a teacher.   3. The library is over there.   4. Are you not a student?   5. Which one is the post office?   6. That is her dictionary, isn't it?   7. That person's desk is over there.   8. Tanaka's watch is expensive, isn't it?   9. Those people were university students.   10. The person over there is the company president, isn't he?   11. The bookseller is a foreigner.   12. We are not Japanese people.

PAGE 49

1. Your friend is in the cafeteria now.   2. Where is the lavatory?   3. I do not have a car.   4. She was in Tokyo last week.   5. The students were not in the classroom yesterday.   6. Who is in that room?   7. This bike is not his.   8. Both the employees and the company president are in the office.   9. Is the wastebasket also in the lavatory?   10. Those people were in the post office yesterday morning.   11. The restaurant is over there, isn't it?   12. Both the bank and the library are there.

PAGE 50

1. Are you going to the library today?   2. Last night I did not go to the cafeteria.   3. The company president went to Tokyo by plane, right?   4. Older sister returns by subway every day.   5. Last month everyone came by train.   6. Let[s go by boat next year.   7. You came with older brother, didn't you?   8. I don't have time now.   9. Did your younger sister return already?   10. Did your friend return to China by plane?   11. Did your husband go to last night's meeting?   12. Tanaka will return to Sapporo tomorrow.

PAGE 51

1. What are you doing now?   2. His parents are living in Osaka.   3. She is writing a letter in [her] room.   4. Older brother and father were running together.   5. Please sit over there with your friend.   6. Everyone has returned to their homes already.   7. Won't you please study a little bit?   8. I will go to the library, but I will not study.   9. Tanaka was standing over there this morning.   10. They (fem.) are still taking a break.   11. Will you please sing that song?   12. I was not working at the bank.

PAGE 52

1. Tomorrow is a holiday, so please rest.   2. Can you speak Japanese?   3. Since you are sick, please don't go to the office.   4. Can't you go to next month's meeting?   5. She cannot sing.   6. Can you wait a little more?   7. Please don't buy it, because it is expensive.   8. Why did you not go downtown?   9. There is no time, so please don't eat yet.   10. Please don't speak with friends in the classroom.   11. I don't have a car, so I will go by train.   12. He cannot speak English, so he was speaking in Japanese.

(Continued on next page.)

PAGE 78

1. What kind of person is Tanaka?   2. I am living in a small apartment.   3. The company president is a stylish person, isn't he?   4. Was last night's meeting late?   5. What kind of people are in this university?

PAGE 79

1. What time did Tanaka come this morning?   2. I think the company president is going to Hawaii.   3. I don't think he will wait until 8:00.   4. I think he already phoned.
5. Mother did not do the shopping yet.

PAGE 80

1. I went downtown and shopped.   2. When I go to Hawaii, I stay at a friend's house.   3. I like watching movies.
4. Mother went there [and came back].   5. I think camping is fun.

PAGE 81

1. Who is the person who is sitting over there?   2. I think I want to go to a movie tonight.   3. I think I want to study with friends.   4. Who was the person who spoke in the classroom?   5. I didn't want to do anything yesterday.

PAGE 82

1. Is it okay to speak [with you] for a moment?   2. Is it okay not to phone until tomorrow?   3. I is not okay to eat in the bookstore.   4. I have to speak with the company president.   5. I have to take (drink) medicine every day.
6. It is okay to go home already.

PAGE 83

1. Is your car big?   2. Yesterday's test was difficult.
3. Today is extremely cold.   4. Her older sister is beautiful, but she is not very easy-going.   5. Tanaka is a lively person.
6. What kind of apartment do you live in?   7. It is convenient, but it is not particularly cheap.   8. She became sick this morning.   9. Father likes him, so he made him rich.
10. I had a lot of work, so it became late.   11. That child is extremely clever.

PAGE 84

1. There are both orange flowers and yellow flowers.
2. Practice makes perfect.   3. She said she likes apples.
4. I cannot do the shopping, because I don't have money.
5. I think this is not the library.   6. She said she went to Japan.   7. I went to a Tokyo department store, but I did not buy anything.   8. He said that they were not eating with friends.   9. I think his Japanese is not particularly skillful.   10. What did you do today?   11. This morning I ate breakfast (a meal) and went to school.

PAGE 85

1. I didn't go with [my] friends to the restaurant, because I didn't want to eat Japanese food.   2. What time do you think you want to eat?   3. I think we have to phone by 4:00.   4. Is it okay to telephone already?   5. You have to try hard!   6. Do you think it is okay to smoke tobacco here?   7. Is it okay not to do anything?   8. It is not okay for your friend to drive.   9. Your father must come.
10. I have to study both today and tomorrow.

PAGE 86

1. When it became winter, I skied.   2. That person is Japanese and cannot [speak] English.   3. They are working with all their might.   4. The company president said he has [some] extremely important business.   5. She is truly pretty.   6. I think I want to go to a movie tonight, but won't you please go with [me]?   7. I'm looking forward to it.   8. Who is the pretty woman who is working in the post office?   9. Today I think I don't want to do anything.

PAGE 87

1. Shall we eat ice cream?   2. Yesterday's test was hard, wasn't it!   3. This apartment is not particularly convenient.
4. Please clean the apartment.   5. The orange car is mine.
6. He said Americans always eat sandwiches.   7. He went to San Francisco, but he did not go to Los Angeles.
8. When I was watching television, I ate popcorn.

PAGE 88

1. Older brother is living in New York, but he studied in France.   2. I hitchhiked up to the mountains and camped.
3. When I go to Hawaii, I stay in a Honolulu hotel.
4. Mr. White said his Spanish friend is coming next week.
5. The person reading the L.A. Times now is Mr. Smith.
6. The Hawaiian wearing the white sweater watched the movie called "Stars Wars" before coming. (watched and came)

PAGE 89

1. Tanaka is a lively person, isn't he?   2. What kind of apartment do you live in?   3. It is convenient, but it is not very big.   4. Today became hot quickly.   5. The man over there is working with all his might.   6. The meeting was not interesting at all!   7. Do you like Japanese food?
8. What is your favorite color?   9. When older brother returned home yesterday, what did he do?   10. He said the department head bought a new car.   11. I don't think she can sing. (or She doesn't think she can sing.)   12. I think he said his car is red.

PAGE 90

1. He did not go to work today.   2. I think that person did not come to the office.   3. Last night's meeting was not long and [therefore it was] good.   4. That book is not particularly interesting.   5. I went to grandfather's place Saturday.   6. She works at the university every day.
7. What do you think you want?   8. He said he needs a pencil.   9. That person said he is looking for the station.
10. I went to the bookstore and bought the book that mother requested.   11. Is it okay to go home already?
12. I have to go to school again on Monday.

PAGE 91

1. Professor Smith's older sister is living in Hawaii.   2. My camera broke (became bad).   3. I got sick because I ate a bad-tasting hamburger.   4. Is the person wearing the orange sweater your friend?   5. He is working in an American bank.   6. Tomorrow I will go to the department store and buy a Mickey Mouse watch.   7. My friend is studying in a French university.   8. I think I want to go to the supermarket when lunch is finished. (Lunch ends and I want to go to the supermarket, I think.)   9. Mother went downtown by bus.   10. Did you order steak and salad?   11. Is it okay to smoke tobacco here?   12. I went to the movie theatre and saw a movie called "Cinderella."

PAGE 92

1. That pen is $10.45, and it is expensive.   2. He is Swedish and speaks French and German.   3. Is the person who is not skiing now sick?   4. I love ice cream and eat it every day.   5. Shall we go to a snack shop and eat a sandwich?
6. Did you go [and come back] by taxi?   7. There was a sale, so Mother went to the supermarket.   8. I can't drive the car, because there is no gasoline.   9. How far (up to what page) did you read?   10. I think the person who is listening to the radio is Mexican.   11. Smith and Brown are travelling in Europe.   12. I had dinner at the hotel restaurant.